Quarterly Essay

CONTENTS

Quarterly Essay is published four times a year by Black Inc., an imprint of Schwartz Media Pty Ltd. Publisher: Morry Schwartz.

ISBN 978-1-86395-311-5 ISSN 1832-0953

Subscriptions – 1 year (4 issues): $49 within Australia incl. GST. Outside Australia $79. 2 years (8 issues): $95 within Australia incl. GST. Outside Australia $155.
Payment may be made by Mastercard, Visa or Bankcard, or by cheque made out to Schwartz Media. Payment includes postage and handling.

To subscribe, fill out and post the subscription card, or subscribe online at:

www.quarterlyessay.com

Correspondence and subscriptions should be addressed to the Editor at:

Black Inc. Level 5, 289 Flinders Lane Melbourne VIC 3000 Australia
Phone: 61 3 9654 2000 / Fax: 61 3 9654 2290
Email:
quarterlyessay@blackincbooks.com (editorial)
subscribe@blackincbooks.com (subscriptions)

Editor: Chris Feik / Management: Sophy Williams
Publicity: Elisabeth Young / Design: Guy Mirabella
Production Co-ordinator: Caitlin Yates

PREFACE

I've been tasked with writing about the election and the markets in the United States this last year. Writing about the recent past is always difficult. Lack of perspective *et cetera*. Writing about the present, one as head-swivelling and gob-smacking as this stretch of time, even worse. Imagine a pot of eels being boiled. Not that I've ever seen eels being boiled, but I'm told that not only do they seethe mightily, as you would expect, but if you turn the heat up too quickly, the eels make heroic leaps for freedom, onto the floor. You have to scramble to gather them up and put them back into the pot. Each day of this last year has brought a fresh scramble to understand events. Here in New York, we've see-sawed between hope and despair, with anxiety our default position. And the eels are still seething, leaping.

AMERICAN REVOLUTION

The Fall of Wall Street and the Rise of Barack Obama

Kate Jennings

WHAT WERE THEY THINKING?

On 1 January, *New York Times* columnist Bob Herbert rang in the new year by remembering an old one: "It seems impossible that 1968, the most incredible year of a most incredible decade, was 40 years ago ... One of the astonishing things about 1968 was how quickly each shocking, consciousness-altering event succeeded the last, leaving no time for people to reorient themselves." Like this past year, 1968 was a presidential election year, and the country was in the midst of an unpopular, polarising war. The North Vietnamese launched the Tet offensive late in January, small people in pyjamas dramatically and successfully challenging the might of the US armed forces, and President Johnson found himself similarly challenged by Eugene McCarthy, a cerebral senator from Minnesota who wanted to negotiate the end of the war. When McCarthy won 42 per cent of the New Hampshire primary vote, the nation became as electrified as it has been by Barack Obama. Bobby Kennedy decided to jump into the race and a traumatised Johnson abandoned it. As Herbert wrote, "Euphoria reigned among young people, and those opposed to the war, and those who believed that people of ordinary good will could change the world." The euphoria lasted four days. Dr Martin Luther King Jr was assassinated; in reaction, riots roiled the country, whole neighbourhoods burned. And then Bobby Kennedy was murdered. By the tiniest of margins, Richard Nixon and Spiro Agnew won the general elections.

A transformative year, unsettlingly similar to 2008, when young people and people of ordinary good will again believed they could change, if not the world, then the United States. In Herbert's opinion, hope died with the bullet that killed RFK, but in my three decades here, I've always found Americans to be the most optimistic of people. That is, until the Bush administration came to power and set about systematically abusing its executive authority.

Apart from the obvious — engaging in two wars, in the process bank-rupting the country morally as well as financially — the Bush administration told so many flat-out lies, deregulated so many industries, fired so many experienced people from government agencies, made so many end-runs around the constitution, destroyed so many checks and balances, ignored so many rules of law, that opponents didn't know where to start fighting the good fight. If the Supreme Court could not make the admin-istration adhere to the Geneva Convention and stop practising torture, what chance did we have of addressing any number of gross illegalities and inequities? Instead, we sank into despair. The country's best impulses were traduced.

All of this was done deliberately. As an epigraph to his damning book *The Wrecking Crew*, Thomas Frank uses a quote from muckraker journalist Lincoln Steffens's 1931 autobiography. In it, a federal politician describes how he and his colleagues piled on the harm and outrage rather than perpetrating a single injustice that would be pounced on and set straight. Said the poli-tician of this diabolic strategy, "We know that public despair is possible and that is good for politics." The kind of immoral, carpet-bagger, screw-you politics that Vice President Dick Cheney made into an art form.

I've asked friends who lived through the Nixon era, known for perfidy, whether these last eight years were worse. Much worse, they always replied. Always on their minds, always intruding. However, when I mentioned the similarity of this year to 1968, they were surprised. Then again, they were preoccupied with making sense of events, wracked with worry that a Democrat wouldn't be voted into the White House on 4 November and we couldn't begin undoing the harm and outrage. And no one ever wants to dwell on assassination, although those dark thoughts emerged, most especially when we observed Barack Obama surrounded tightly by secret-service men in a formation that brought to mind the Praetorian Guard.

On 1 January 2008, an article in the *New York Times* was headed, "What if Iowa Settles Nothing for Democrats?" It referred to the primary vote just two days away. Another article noted that sales of previously owned homes had nudged up in December 2007 but not enough to improve the broader picture of "record-high foreclosures and harder-to-get credit." Detroit was worried but would be fine if gas prices came down. A business writer began a piece with this sentence: "Like baseball or the weather, the economy can be a difficult thing to predict." He went on to say how surprised everyone was in 2007 to see the subprime housing crisis spread to the financial sector. For the basketball fans among us, a rhetorical question was asked on the sport pages: "Could It Get Worse for the Knicks? Amazingly, Yes."

As we know, Iowa didn't settle anything for the Democrats. The price of oil soared, and Detroit, myopically dependent on SUV gas-guzzlers, found itself in more trouble than ever before. Given a shove by the subprime crisis, the shadow banking system – a teetering pyramid of trillions of dollars' worth of unregulated derivatives – collapsed, the credit markets seized, and the US economy fell off a cliff. Actually, as more than one commentator noted, at first it pedalled furiously in mid-air like Wile E. Coyote and then fell like a stone. Other countries followed suit. Global financial markets = global financial crisis. All of which was foretold by a number of financial experts not in thrall to former Federal Reserve chief

Alan Greenspan and the free markets. And the Knicks went from abysmal to putridly abysmal, until the Dolans, owners of the team, finally fired coach Isaiah Thomas, a man who could give lessons on arrogance to investment bankers. Just like the US economy, it will take years to rebuild the Knicks. "When things can't continue, they stop." A piece of sports wisdom which could be the epitaph for 2008.

Barack Obama won Iowa, thoroughly upsetting the assumption that Hillary Clinton would become the nominee because Obama, although talented, was too young, too inexperienced; his time would come. He then lost in New Hampshire to Clinton, and we started on what Jon Stewart on the Comedy Channel's *The Daily Show* called "The Long, Flat, Seemingly Endless Bataan Death March to the White House." Obama triumphed, but not before friends fell out and spouses shouted at each other over the candidates' respective merits. Not-so-civil war.

The US election season was turned over – tilled, ploughed, excavated, bulldozed – by pundits until all that was left was dust. As the daily emails from the Obama campaign reminded me, we went at it for twenty-two months. Everyone was having a say – and not without cause. First, a woman and a black man running against each other for the Democratic nomination for the president of the United States; and then the black guy – the young black guy – triumphing to go up against the old white guy, John McCain. Who would have thought?

In New York, we all became political junkies: the cabbie, the doorman, the sushi-maker. And we shook our heads more than once that after all these years of waiting, Democrats had both a woman and an African-American running. I voted for Hillary Clinton in the primaries. She is an extraordinary woman and would have made an excellent president. I love Bill Clinton, too, even though he broke our hearts when he couldn't keep it zipped back when he was president, knowing full well that Republicans would set on him like jackals if they got a whiff of sexual shenanigans. He self-immolated, destroyed his presidency – and our hopes. And then, during the 2008 primaries, he went ape, ego in full throttle, unable to control his feelings about Obama taking his place in the spotlight. If Hillary had won, what would she have done with Bill? Sent him to the North Pole in the hope that his temper would cool and his you-know-what would freeze and drop off?

I changed my allegiance to Obama when I heard him give his race speech – "A More Perfect Union" – in Philadelphia. One of my trades is speech-writing. (I learned it on Wall Street from the best – ex-Republican Party operatives.) I am in complete awe of that speech because it contained much more than the usual pap about hope, the obligatory lines about race. Obama even quoted Faulkner: "The past isn't dead and buried. In fact, it isn't even past." He might only be forty-seven years old, but anyone smart enough to give that speech will be smart enough to surround himself with people who won't truck in conventional wisdom. Also, he is not beholden to interest groups in the way that time-serving pols inevitably are.

And Hillary Clinton, for all her smarts, made a huge mistake, running a twentieth-century top-down, status-quo campaign in the twenty-first century. She ignored what Howard Dean had already discovered in 2004: the internet is a potent "viral" funding tool. It's also a matchless way to energise a vast grassroots voting base. "Did they sleep through the 2003–04 election cycle?" asked one of Howard Dean's advisers.

What was Clinton thinking in dismissing Dean's pioneering internet fundraising effort? For that matter, what was New York State's governor Elliot Spitzer thinking when he crossed state lines to have sex with a prostitute, allowing investigators to wiretap his phone calls? We'd hoped that Spitzer, who successfully took on the banks and the insurance companies when he was attorney-general, would be able to reform our state government, one of the most corrupt in the nation. Instead he is spending his days seeing a marriage counsellor and running his family's real-estate company. What was John Edwards, who would have made a great secretary of labour in an Obama administration, thinking when he had an affair with a campaign worker, which he excused by saying it happened when his wife was in remission from cancer? Bizarrely, he finished his *mea culpa* by telling us not to blame his family for his behaviour. Honey, you screwed up all by yourself, but you also screwed with our good faith in running as a presidential nominee. What was Christopher Dodd, another shining Democratic Party presidential hopeful, thinking when he allowed himself to be put on the VIP list at mortgage lender Countrywide Financial? Now he's stonewalling, denying any wrongdoing: "I never sought any special treatment. I never was offered any special treatment." What was John McCain thinking when he chose someone as blatantly unqualified as Sarah Palin as his running mate? And what were banking CEOs thinking when they allowed their proprietary trading desks to go hog wild with credit default swaps? ("Cold dogshit," as one trader called them.) I could go on. Equal-opportunity, non-partisan, meritocratic arrogance.

I want to digress here, with purpose, by bringing up Clay Shirky. He has written a book called *Here Comes Everybody: The Power of Organizing Without Organizations*, which a techie friend, Dean, thrust upon me. I tried very hard to read it, mainly because I hate being thought of as an old fart by know-it-all techies. Over half the book involves an interminable story about a young woman who loses her cell phone and how a "movement," so to speak, of her friends and acquaintances was able to retrieve it via social-networking sites on the web.

Plumbing new depths of inanity, or so I thought. Dean and I argue about the web. He thinks I'm a dinosaur because I like clear sentences and well-constructed arguments. I counter that he can't spell, knows zip about punctuation, and wouldn't recognise coherent reasoning if he fell over it. He is full of infectious enthusiasm for the internet and its possibilities. Actually, as am I. But I don't do any social networking on the web, and I rarely read blogs; there are only so many hours in the day.

The last book I read about the internet was Andrew Keen's *The Cult of the Amateur: How Today's Internet is Killing Our Culture*. This book seemed to me to be spot on. Communities on the web are, by and large, disastrously narcissistic, eye-crossingly moronic, and don't give a tinker's damn about piracy or plagiarism or fact-based editing. On these sites, truth is extremely relative.

Qualms about this vast, ever-growing mosh-pit of noxious mediocrity are usually shrugged off by web true-believers. No problem, they say, the cream will always rise to the top. Doomsayers like Andrew Keen and myself think it's impossible for cream to rise when communication channels are clogged with half-baked opinions, illiterate rants and skateboarding dogs.

Okay, that's the downside of "here comes everybody." The barbarian hordes. Punctuation cretins. Still, I wanted to understand this Shirky fellow – he's the bright boy of the moment – so I watched a video of a seminar on the future of the internet where Shirky was a participant. Lots of preening – we're talking Young Turks here, very pleased with themselves – but interesting nonetheless.

Shirky argued that, because of the web, we are experiencing an enormous cognitive surplus – and right through history, whenever there are surpluses of any kind, there is change. In his view, the web has pushed huge amounts of flexibility out into society. You don't have to ask for help or permission to attempt anything. And that being the case, the internet has many futures filled with diverse surprises.

Now, back to Obama. One of those diverse surprises – and the *upside* of "here comes everybody" – was the election of Barack Obama. He became the president-elect in part because of his even temperament, obvious intelligence and ability to give effortless, nuanced speeches. Not to forget his charisma. That smile! Melts glaciers quicker than global warming. The man is a sport of nature. And also because of his extraordinary fundraising machine that utilised the very flexibility to which Shirky refers.

Behind Obama's run was a group of Silicon Valley brainiacs who borrowed the subscription model that the software business had been using since the internet bubble burst. With funds seriously diminished, many tech companies couldn't pony up large sums to buy software. So it was made available on a subscription basis. Small sums over time.

This idea was applied to fundraising for Obama. Instead of giving one lump sum to a campaigner, usually cajoled out of you in a living room, you joined My.BarackObama.com and committed yourself to a certain sum over a period of time. And you got your friends to join through MySpace or LinkedIn or other social-networking sites. Netroots.

The momentum grew. And grew. End result: by the time Obama won the Democratic nomination his campaign was bringing in US$2 million a day, $200 million in the last year. By comparison, Clinton's campaign was deep in debt. And Obama's staff had gone from zero employees to 700. And the staff was on the ground in all the states, raring to go. Up against John McCain, his campaign chest filled to bursting. In September, he raised an astronomical $150 million. Nobody had seen anything like it. As well, "here comes everybody" is changing government itself, with hubs of power, courtesy of web flexibility, moving outside the Beltway.

This is "here comes everybody" in the very best sense. But who are the everybodys? At first, young people. The word on them for a long time was that they were beyond apathetic. Blobs intent on instant gratification and focused only on their careers, or so baby-boomers grumbled. A wondrous thing that they have been motivated to care, to become involved, to think that their votes matter. And an early initiation in grassroots politics can mean a lifetime of commitment to the greater good.

More interesting, though, is that a whole new voting bloc has been mobilised via technology. As my editor puts it, "the Obama people are getting virtual voters to real booths. Technologically enhanced democracy." He elaborated further: "People are upgrading to Obama-style politics, which is much more satisfying than old-style spectatorial politics. More connected. A more perfect union, to use the name of Obama's race speech in Philadelphia, of candidate and constituency."

What was marvellous about election year 2008 was the historically high levels of people who voted in the primaries and the even larger numbers who registered to vote on 4 November. The latter number among Democrats tripled or quadrupled in many states. Voting in the US isn't compulsory, which means only a pathetic fraction votes, but 2008 was different. This was despite the usual Republican efforts to disenfranchise people who would vote Democrat. For example, some states began asking voters for a government-issued photo ID, which minority groups often don't have. In one conspicuous application of this rule, a busload of aged nuns was turned away from voting in the primaries.

Still, given the appalling state of the nation, Americans are taking a risk in electing Obama. Will he be a wise, measured statesman or are we getting a pig in a poke? An idealistic intellectual? Nervousness and second thoughts were the order of the day right through the primaries, but his performance in the debates against McCain, his reaction to the economic crisis, his refusal to be baited by the slurs from the right, and the discipline of his campaign soothed us.

A digression here on the idiom "pig in a poke." A poke is a Middle Ages word for a bag. Meat was scarce back then, so unscrupulous people would put cats in a bag and sell the wriggling sack as a suckling pig. Strangely enough, the idiom and the con is much the same across many cultures. Cats in bags the world over. Some would say that a 47-year-old idealistic intellectual is the very definition of a pig in a poke. Pigs, with and without lipstick, featured prominently in politics in 2008.

HOLD FIRMLY, WITHOUT WAVERING

Perhaps too much was made of gender and race in the primaries. Two very capable *people* ran for the Democratic Party nomination. But let's not forget that for the first time in the US a woman ran and nearly won the nomination at a time when the representation of women in the Senate and the House of Representatives is woeful: 13 out of 100 in the Senate; 61 out of 435 in the House.

And let's not forget that a black man ran and won the Democratic Party nomination at a time when *one out of three* black men between the ages of twenty and twenty-nine is incarcerated, according to Human Rights Watch. Men who will spend the rest of their lives disenfranchised, of course, although my point is that Obama made his run in a society that tolerates a high degree of institutionalised racism. Another statistic: Obama was the only black senator, a number that hasn't changed in forty years.

The Democratic National Convention was perfectly orchestrated, no small feat given how fractious and self-defeating Democrats can be. Hillary Clinton was superb. And gracious: "Barack Obama is my candidate. And he must be our president ... Whether you voted for me, or voted for Barack, the time is now to unite as a single party with a single purpose. We are on the same team, and none of us can sit on the sidelines. This is a fight for the future. And it's a fight we must win." Even Bill, that old wag, delivered the goods. With a single clever sentence – "What a year we Democrats have had!" – he acknowledged the emotions generated by the arduous primary battle and pushed the Democratic Party beyond divisiveness. He went on to say, "Hillary told us in no uncertain terms that she'll do everything she can to elect Barack Obama. That makes two of us. Actually that makes eighteen million of us – because, like Hillary, I want all of you who supported her to vote for Barack Obama." Joe Biden was as expected – a little hesitant and bumbling but a knowledgeable, experienced regular Joe. I've always liked Biden because he can be impudent; he has a spark in his eye.

Obama purposefully tamped down the soaring rhetoric. No "fierce urgency of now" or "righteous wind at our back." Instead, he projected a strong, steady image, one to which he has hewed: "America, we are better than these last eight years. We are a better country than this ... America, we cannot turn back. Not with so much work to be done. Not with so many children to educate, and so many veterans to care for. Not with an economy to fix and cities to rebuild and farms to save. Not with so many families to protect and so many lives to mend. America, we cannot turn back. We cannot walk alone. At this moment, in this election, we must pledge once more to march into the future. Let us keep that promise – that American promise – and in the words of scripture hold firmly, without wavering, to the hope that we confess."

I admit that I'm a sucker for an elegant word or two of scripture. To write this, I watched Obama's acceptance speech again. What struck me is that it wasn't just the scripture that was elegant: Obama has an elegance of mind and body rarely, if ever, seen in politics. (JFK could be eloquent but exuded virility, not elegance.) The word on Obama is that he is courteous. He listens. He doesn't like to disagree, not to your face. And he's also ruthlessly pragmatic. The inflammatory nature of the 21 July *New Yorker* cover where Obama and Michelle are depicted fist-bumping – a power jab – in the Oval Office, he kitted up as a Muslim and she as a *Soul on Ice* '60s radical, made people overlook the article on Obama inside. If you have doubts about the man's toughness, read it. The likelihood of him being chewed up and spat out by Washington is low.

Several days after the Democratic Convention, John McCain announced that Sarah Palin, the Governor of Alaska, would be his running mate. She flattened the Democrats, landing with a thump on them like Dorothy's house in Munchkinland. Insult to injury, Palin also has a penchant for ruby-red shoes, in her case Naughty Monkey stilettos. In case you don't know the brand, Naughty Monkey shoes have "a playful and bright color palette" that "offers a variety of fast paced, ever-changing styles for today's junior woman's needs. Naughty Monkey ... allows any young woman to express her individual style, attitude and youthfulness." They are available from a website called – I kid you not – The Shoe Fairy.

I'm not one of those who hate, hate, hate Palin. I just find her to be about the most annoying politician of all time, which is saying something. After the novelty of her "betchas" and "gotchas" and flirty ways wore off, Palin's "individual style" came to be a minus for McCain, but not before she invigorated the Far Right and gave credence to any amount of cesspit lies and crude exaggerations about Obama. We underestimated her and her steely ambition, mistaking ignorance for stupidity, just as we (mis)underestimated George W. Bush.

In the vice-presidential debate, Sarah Palin was asked her view of the vice president's job. In reply she took the current vice president, Dick Cheney, as her role model by saying, "We have a lot of flexibility in there" under the constitution. And she declared that she was "thankful that the constitution would allow a bit more authority given to the vice president also, if that vice president so chose to exert it."

Later she got into trouble by telling an interviewer that the vice president runs the Senate. (The vice president can cast a tie-breaking vote if the Senate is locked.) Syntax and gaffes aside, she brought back with a rush the underlying theme of the last eight years: the unprecedented abuse of executive power, masterminded by Dick Cheney, who perversely was inspired by Watergate, from which he took the outlandish lesson that Congress was too powerful and the president not powerful enough. We all know his sins: removing checks and balances from the executive branch, misleading us about weapons of mass destruction, creating illegal prison camps where detainees are tortured, illegally wiretapping US citizens, and creating an energy policy that favoured his friends in the oil industry.

At the beginning of the Bush era, Cheney gave a few interviews, but long ago called a halt to that kind of accountability. We were able to glimpse his mindset when David Addington, his chief of staff, was hauled in front of the House Judiciary Committee to testify about the administration's stand on torture. Known as Cheney's Cheney – Darth Vader's Darth Vader, Machiavelli's Machiavelli – Addington has been glimpsed even less often than his boss, so seeing him appear under subpoena was like watching a vampire being forced into the sunlight. Sitting slumped and scratching his moustache – it's a wonder he didn't give his balls a hitch – he snarled and growled his way through the committee's questions, rudely stonewalling at every turn. On full display was not just his hostility to being asked questions by those he obviously considered his inferiors, but also his utter contempt for the process of government. This was the man responsible both for the idea of an imperial presidency and the bizarre notion that the vice president isn't part of either the executive or legislative branch.

At the end of the session, Addington was asked by a congressman about water-boarding but refused to answer on the grounds that al-Qaeda might be watching. "I'm glad they finally have a chance to see you, Mr Addington," joked the congressman. To which he shot back, "I'm sure you are pleased."

The insidious work of Cheney and Addington was on display in an infinitely sad, infinitely distressing documentary on the Bush administration's torture policy that was shown on some public television stations but not, alas, in Addington's hometown, Washington. Titled *Torturing Democracy*, the documentary is one of those pieces of film-making that set you back on your heels even when you are familiar with the material. One line I hadn't heard before: "What constitutes torture is perception. If the prisoner dies you're doing it wrong." (The documentary can be watched at <torturingdemocracy.org>.)

Also released in 2008 was another chilling documentary, *Boogie Man*, on the life and deeds of Lee Atwater, a Peck's Bad Boy who institutionalised dirty-tricks campaigning. A Gollum in chinos and button-down-collar shirts. A Gollum who was master of the salacious tidbit. A Gollum who had two potent insights: perception is reality and people vote their fears, not their hopes. Dirty tricks, of course, have been around forever in politics, but Atwater came along at a time when the Republicans were in the ascendancy, and he pumped their tyres full of air. First as a political operative for Ronald Reagan and George H. Bush and then as chairman of the Republican National Committee, he rewrote the GOP playbook by legitimising dirty tricks: you could accuse anyone of anything right out in the open. Unleashed a world of slurs, a world of hurt. Atwater masterminded, for example, the infamous Willie Horton ad that sunk Michael Dukakis in the 1988 presidential election; Dukakis never knew what hit him.

One revelation: Papa and Mama Bush, not knowing what to do with their tail-chasing, beer-guzzling son, Dubbya, handed him over to Atwater to babysit. Their wayward sprog glommed onto Atwater's lessons like a succubus and went back to Texas with Atwater mentoree Karl Rove to trounce Governor Ann Richards by alleging she was lesbian. Lee Atwater begat Karl Rove, David Addington, Rush Limbaugh, the Swift Boat campaign and the "fair and balanced" Fox News. His methods begat unfettered presidential power.

Atwater was a Southern boy from an impoverished family with a lot to prove to the world. He was also a classic example of a campaign rat, only interested in process and winning, not ideology. Zero capacity for introspection. Although he destroyed careers, he was well liked because he did it with an energetic and cheeky insouciance, which led to him being known as the "happy hatchet man." The documentary about his life is called *Boogie Man* because Atwater once played backup for Percy Sledge and hung out with B.B. King. Here's Atwater finessing the GOP's Southern strategy:

> You start out in 1954 by saying, "Nigger, nigger, nigger." By 1968 you can't say "nigger" – that hurts you. Backfires. So you say stuff like forced bussing, states' rights and all that stuff. You're getting so abstract now [that] you're talking about cutting taxes, and all these

things you're talking about are totally economic things and a by-product of them is [that] blacks get hurt worse than whites.

And subconsciously maybe that is part of it. I'm not saying that. But I'm saying that if it is getting that abstract, and that coded, that we are doing away with the racial problem one way or the other. You follow me — because obviously sitting around saying, "We want to cut this," is much more abstract than even the bussing thing, and a hell of a lot more abstract than "Nigger, nigger."

BRIGHT, GUILTY WORLD

And now for the backdrop against which the cabbie, the doorman and the sushi-maker are bending each other's ears with such ferocity: "It's a bright, guilty world." These are lines spoken by the Orson Welles character, Black Irish, in the movie *The Lady from Shanghai*. Black Irish gets caught up with a nefarious bunch when he falls for Rita Hayworth and has a hard time keeping his moral compass. He and his companions dock their yacht in Acapulco. Black Irish looks around at the languorous environment and says, "It's a bright, guilty world."

It's a bright, guilty world where I live. I'm just up the street from 15 Central Park West, where an apartment was sold for a record-setting US$46 million. The building itself isn't a glass tower – it's a hulking pastiche of pre-war styles to give residents a feeling of solidity. And the way the markets are going, they might need that illusion.

Here's a startling statistic: in 1993, 1 per cent of families in the US pocketed 14 per cent of the nation's income. By 2006, that slice had grown to 23 per cent. If you dissect that figure even further, 15,000 families in the top .01 per cent drew 5.5 per cent of the nation's total income. It's a bright, guilty world.

A story. When I worked on Wall Street I came into contact with extreme and often ludicrous wealth, but that was some time ago. Early in 2008, I was invited to dine at Cipriani's, which is catty-corner from the Plaza Hotel, recently transformed into luxury condos that sold for prices nearly as stupendous as those at 15 CPW, even the ones with views of air shafts.

The crowd at Cipriani's is polished to a fare-thee-well. Burnished. Their feet rarely touch the pavement. The food is mediocre at best – I'll take a meal at Sean's at Bondi over Cipriani's any day – but it is expensive, the point being that its clientele are the sort who can afford to throw away a thousand or two for a modest weekday supper.

My two companions were my dentist and my neurologist. We were chatting in a spirited way when suddenly they both fell silent: a respectful three-second silence. Private-equity king Henry Kravis and his entourage were being seated at the table next to us. I was oblivious to this notable arrival. Instead I was taking in the women in the room. They were all thin – that goes without saying – and every last one had a face that had gone under the knife more than once. To me, they looked not just unnatural but malformed, grotesque.

Feminist that I am, I couldn't resist mentioning this. My dentist then told me about a patient of his who was about to have some wrinkles botox-ed when the dermatologist informed her that after the procedure she wouldn't be able to say the letter "p." I gave a very unladylike cackle and said, "There are women in this room who can't say whole words."

My other companion, the neurologist, usually a light-hearted sort, reprimanded me: "Kate, if you want to be a player on the Upper East Side, you have to work at it." For men, this means staying wealthy and giving money to the right charities in significant amounts, although even that won't guarantee a table at the Four Seasons because the rules of this tribe are inscrutable. For the women, it means approximating the look of youth and maintaining the air of a courtesan. Once upon a time, women had their feet bound or wore corsets so tight they suffered renal failure. Now they endure mutilating face jobs that cause linguistic difficulties. But to the diners at Cipriani's, who keep company only with each other, the women appeared normal. And so it is with bankers: keep company only with people who behave like conger eels and after a while that seems normal.

In the last eight years, many of us were kept sane by watching Jon Stewart's *Daily Show*. While the mainstream press fawned or cowered, the show's satire became an accurate take on reality that was tragic but also surreal.

Here's an example: Stewart asked his White House "correspondent," John Oliver, if there was anything else left for Bush to mess up. To "de-accomplish."

"He knows he can never be the best president," answered Oliver, "but if he works hard, *very* hard, he could still be ..."

Stewart interrupted and suggested, "The worst president?"

"No, Jon," replied Oliver. "The *last* president."

Someone once said to Stewart that he must have a huge research staff to come up with the clips they use. He deadpanned, "We have one intern with a video machine." His material is just sitting there, day in, day out, ripe for the plucking.

As the year progressed and the economic news worsened, the wars in Iraq and Afghanistan receded from public discourse. During the primary battle between Clinton and Obama, the Iraq war was a critical issue because Hillary had initially supported the war and never could bring herself to say she might have made a mistake. Despite Iraq's ongoing fragility, Bush's "surge" strategy received loud huzzahs. And then Nouri al-Maliki, the Iraqi prime minister, called for a timed withdrawal identical to the one proposed by Obama, followed by all sixteen heads of the US intelligence units in Afghanistan saying that things had gone terribly wrong, more troops were needed there. Overnight, or so it seemed, talk about the success of the surge disappeared.

The only time that the six-year-long wars, still parsed as the War on Terror, impinged was when we had to take our shoes off at the airport. Everyone complains about airport security because of the inconvenience and the sometimes peculiar interpretation of what can be taken on planes but also because of its patent ineffectuality. Every now and again a reporter loads up with knives, screwdrivers and the like, sails through airport security, and publishes an exposé. New Yorkers certainly don't feel safe, not with a nuclear reactor a couple of miles up the Hudson River and unguarded container terminals surrounding Manhattan.

I was roundly reminded of the War on Terror on my way back from a trip to Australia when I tried to bring home a snow globe in my carry-on bag. Making the whole episode even more incongruous than usual, this was no ordinary snow globe. Standing seven inches high, the bottom half is a replica of the White House decorated with camouflage streaks. In the globe itself, standing on barrels of oil and piles of auto tyres, are three dogs. The largest canine is an attack dog – a Staffordshire terrier. A poodle is trying to climb up on the Staffie's back, and a Cairn is sniffing the Staffie's bottom. When shaken, a blizzard of tiny red, white and blue stars obscures the dogs as well as the bones and poop littering the bottom of the globe. This fanciful work came from the fertile mind of Australian artist Fiona Hall.

The globe was a present for my birthday back in 2004 from my great friends, Brook and John, an Aussie couple who knew I was writing a book about my two border terriers – a book that was also larded with cheeky political commentary about the Bush administration and reflections on the effect of the War on Terror on life in New York City. The globe not only literally encapsulated all my preoccupations but did it with the kind of wacky humour that tickles me. As presents go, they'd hit a bullseye. They sent me a photo, and we promptly dubbed it "The Dogs of War." However, glitches in the globe's manufacture delayed its delivery to Brook and John. We decided that because of its fragility, I should bring it home to New York after my next trip to Australia rather than entrusting it to the post. Several years passed before I made the journey, so it wasn't until the middle of 2008 that I took possession.

I had arrived three hours early for the flight as per instructions. I was looking forward to breakfast in the airline's lounge, but as my carry-on bag exited the X-ray machine, a security officer pounced. "You have a snow globe?" she asked.

"Yes. You should see it. It's a *beauty*." See it she did. We teased the globe out of its tight Styrofoam packing, and she gave it a cursory examination, her face an absolute blank. In fact, she was magnificently unimpressed. Then again, the things she sees emerge from luggage every day would probably boggle the mind.

"It's called 'The Dogs of War,'" I helpfully informed her, but thought better of telling her that the scene depicted was the reason she had her job.

"Madam, whatever you call it, it's still a snow globe. It contains liquid. You should have packed it in your check-in luggage. Too late for that now. I have to confiscate it."

"Confiscate it? You can't do that!" I explained that the globe was fragile, which was why I hadn't put it in a suitcase. No response. Brick wall.

"Can I see your manager?" I asked. We threaded our way through people replacing laptops in cases and spare change in pockets to a young man standing behind a high desk.

"Snow globe," said the security officer, presenting it to him.

"'The Dogs of War,'" I said. We were eyeball to eyeball. He looked at me, at the globe, and tried not to smile. Ah, he got the humour and maybe even the irony that the subject of the snow globe was the very thing that prevented me from taking it on board.

He gave it a shake. Red, white and blue stars fizzed around the barrels of oil and the dogs astride them. "What sort of liquid is in this?" he asked.

I hazarded a guess. "Water?"

"Can we drain it?"

"I don't think so." Again I explained how fragile the snow globe was and also told him about its provenance, the artist's fame. I finished by saying, "It's worth a lot of money," thinking that would be the clincher.

"Sorry. The limit for liquids is 100 millilitres. And that's a big globe." He was an affable fellow, going out of his way not to be offensive. "But you can leave it here for seven days and have someone pick it up. After that, we'll have to destroy it."

"Destroy it? You can't do that! It's a work of art!" I explained that the friends who gave it to me were in Europe. There was no one to fetch it. Or at least no one who was going to trek out to the airport for a snow globe, however witty and whimsical it might be.

He thought for a bit. "Maybe if you see the staff on the plane, they might help," he suggested.

It is not by accident that my dogs are terriers. The snow globe had waited four years for me, and the damn thing was coming on that plane come hell or high water. Off I set, zigzagging through acres of duty-free stalls, trundling down long corridors, queuing at a second security point, finally arriving at the boarding area. No lolling in a lounge for me that day; I was going to need every minute of those three hours.

I explained my predicament to the airline representative at the ticket desk, pleading my case with as much eloquence and good humour as I could muster. "It's a *splendid* globe," I finished. "One of a kind. You can't destroy it."

"Sorry. No can help." I tried again, but she'd shut down. Short of phoning the airline chairman, I was defeated. I was telling myself that I'd given it a good college try when she said, "Look, why don't you ask the security manager to give me a ring." And handed me her extension number.

Back at the security manager's desk, I said, "Me again." And added, "'The Dogs of War,'" just in case he'd forgotten in the last half-hour. "The woman at the boarding desk said to call her." They talked, and he agreed to bring the snow globe to show her.

As we walked along, I asked, "You like dogs?"

"Oh yes! I used to have five chihuahuas, but they all died. I'm taking a break," he replied.

"Five! Oh my!" I told him about my book about my dogs, *Stanley and Sophie*, and confided that I didn't believe in heaven, not for humans, but I did for dogs. How could there not be a heaven for dogs? I was blathering with intent; he was grinning. Now we had a connection: the universal bond of dog-lovers.

At the gate the security manager and airline representative conferred. "Got a bag?" she asked me. We tucked the snow globe in my canvas carry-on along with everything I'd brought to keep me comfortable for the twenty-hour flight to New York. While we did this, she started to mutter,

"I'm gonna lose my job." I began to feel bad, but not *that* bad. Forms were signed and the bag tagged and sent down a chute into the belly of the plane. I thanked the representative and shook hands with the security manager, wishing him luck with future chihuahuas.

No way was that snow globe going to arrive in New York intact. Still, I'd tried. And the irony of the whole affair appealed. At JFK, my heart sank as I watched the bag come banging down the slide onto the carousel, smashing into solid suitcases. I retrieved it, to find the bottom felt damp. Oh well, win some, lose some. As it turned out, the bag had merely been sitting next to something cold, chilling it. Inside, "The Dogs of War" was in one piece and now sits in pride of place in my apartment, a reminder, if I should need one, of what happens when we cry havoc and let slip the dogs of war.

CONSIDER THE BANKER

We all have obsessions, and one of mine, thought strange for someone literary, are the financial instruments known as derivatives that are at the centre of the economic meltdown we are experiencing. Derivatives are commonly defined as a financial contract where the value is derived from an underlying asset. These contracts cover the buying and selling of a wide variety of goods, ranging from currencies and agricultural products to oil and metals to stocks and bonds. They are not inherently bad. Indeed, the commodity markets are based on futures, which is a form of derivative that has been around since the Sumerians. A hog farmer wants to lock in a price for his pork bellies so he isn't exposed to market vagaries. He contracts with a trader to receive a payment in the future for the bellies. Money is made or lost if there is, say, an undersupply caused by swine fever or an oversupply by a bumper crop of piglets.

We've landed in our current mess through the misuse of unregulated derivatives that became ever more ornate, ever more synthetic – frequently called bells-and-whistles securities but more like gimcrack and paste – in the credit markets, which includes the mortgage industry. Credit markets: any market where a loan is made or a bond sold.

My interest came about by accident. I went to work at Merrill Lynch as a speechwriter in the 1990s under the aegis of one of the directors. I needed money because my husband was ill. The boys in the communications department were none too happy to have a fifty-year-old "left-wing bohemian poet," to use their classification, who didn't know a stock from a bond on their hands, and so they fed me to an executive who not only had an alligatorish face but the habits of one. He liked nothing better than to feast on communications staff. "Stay off his radar screen!" – that was the word on him. He terrified them.

The executive had to give a speech in Tokyo to the International Swaps and Derivatives Association, known as ISDA, and I had to write that speech. Armed with a list of the firm's bankers to interview, I was pushed into the deep end of finance. Once the speech was completed, it was distributed, as was the custom, to all the top executives for comments. One of them had been part of a group that had written a white paper on derivatives.

I remember entering his office, bigger than my apartment, and immediately tripping on the Persian carpet. Righting myself, I began the long journey to his desk. He had a highly polished desk and a photograph of his wife, a blonde X-ray, standing in solitary splendour on a credenza behind him. As I approached, he asked, holding up the speech between his thumb and forefinger, "What's a nice young girl like you doing with rubbish like this?"

It was, shall we say, a transformative moment. A defining moment. I could've left his office, left the building, left the firm. But I wasn't young: I was a fifty-year-old with a husband with Alzheimer's. And some might say I'm not even nice – I can take paint off a barn door if the occasion calls for it. As well, I was getting curious about bankers. They weren't, as I'd been led to expect, boring men and women in suits. In fact, underneath those suits, eye-popping emotions. I chose not to be intimidated. I replied, "Let's go over the rubbish." And sat down.

Needless to say, after that excruciating experience, derivatives were imprinted indelibly on my mind. The speech was given in Tokyo and deemed a success. The fearsome executive didn't eat me and spit out the gristle, much to the chagrin of my new colleagues. But when I left Wall Street seven years later and sat down to sort out my thoughts and write a novel about my experience there, I realised the speech *was* rubbish. The critical executive was exactly right because the screed was stuffed with the standard banking frontiers-of-finance, mitts-off line on "innovative" structured products.

Financial-industry family trees – who lands where – are always interesting to those involved. For example, the trading desks of the Financial Products Unit that got the insurance giant AIG into such trouble by venturing into derivatives were staffed by traders from Drexel Burnham

Lambert, the company that went under in the 1980s because Michael Milken and Ivan Boesky pushed the junk-bond envelope. I couldn't resist researching where the two men – the alligatorish executive and the savvy one – are now. The first is now on the do-nothing board of AIG. The other is wearing a white hat at the Financial Stability Institute, which the Basel Committee on Banking Supervision established as a clearing house on worldwide banking regulation.

I began to keep a scrapbook on derivatives. In it went Alan Greenspan's speech to the Futures Industry Association in March of 1999. Derivatives should remain unregulated, he said, despite the "trauma of the past eighteen months." Those months had seen a number of crises, but he was referring in particular to the Long Term Capital Management fiasco. LTCM was a cutting-edge hedge fund heavily weighted in derivatives that went bankrupt in 1998, forcing the government to come to the rescue because so many Wall Street banks had large exposures. Then, on 13 December 2000, a tiny article on the business pages announced the imminent passing of the *Commodities Futures Modernization Act*, which allowed banks to continue to self-regulate derivatives. Brooksley Born, the head of the Commodity Futures Trading Commission, had gone up against Alan Greenspan, Treasury Secretary Robert Rubin and Securities and Exchange Commission head Arthur Levitt for two years after LTCM failed, imploring them to regulate what was known as the "dark markets." She'd also testified in front of Congress seventeen times, to no avail.

The bankers had an ally, Republican Senator Phil Gramm, known latterly for giving John McCain bone-headed economic advice and telling Americans that they are a nation of whiners. As the influential chairman of the Senate Banking Committee, he called for "regulatory relief," saying we "would do well to remember the Lincoln adage that to ask a society to live under old and outmoded laws – and I think you could say the same about regulation – is like asking a man to wear the same clothes he wore as a boy." Even though Brooksley Born is a real fighter – Greenspan and company called her "strident" in public and no doubt worse in private –

she didn't stand a chance against the banking lobby. The *Commodities Futures Modernization Act* was signed into law by Bill Clinton, with a rider inserted by Gramm that allowed derivatives to flourish unchecked with minimal capital requirements – that is, the money banks should have as a backstop if anything goes awry.

We're done for, I can remember thinking, when I read about the passing of the act. Clipped it, pasted it in my scrapbook. In my novel, the main character, a speechwriter like myself, has conversations with a risk manager who bangs on obsessively about the danger of unregulated derivatives, which he thinks, along with global warming, will be the end of us. The speechwriter is more fatalistic: stuff happens. Clearly, I was more aligned with my risk manager than my speechwriter.

I also made my risk manager a moral-hazard fundamentalist, as am I. Moral hazard – another crucial issue that's reared its head in the last six months. I first heard the phrase when I was writing speeches for an executive at J.P. Morgan further along in my Wall Street career. I couldn't believe my ears. Redolent with meaning! So redolent that I used it as the title for my novel. To his amusement, I stopped in my tracks and asked if he had made it up. He explained that it was an insurance industry term – if a house is insured, appropriate care might not be taken to stop it from going up in flames – that had migrated to banking.

When used in connection with banking, moral hazard means, simply, that if bankers know that the government will save their franchise – their bacon – they will become careless in regard to due diligence and risk assessment. The British comedians John Bird and John Fortune have made hay with the term in the popular YouTube skits where they play an obtuse investment banker and an interviewer. The interviewer asks, "Can we talk about moral hazard?"

The banker goes blank: "About what?"

"Moral hazard," repeats the interviewer.

"I know what hazard means," says the banker, "but what's the other word?"

The Bird and Fortune skit ends with the interviewer telling the banker that he hasn't learned anything, and the banker disagrees, saying he has learned that "if you are going to make a cock-up, make sure it is an absolutely enormous cock-up because then the government is going to bail you out." Chuckles all around, but with the financial markets reduced to matchsticks, I've wondered if bankers actually know what hazard means.

The concept of moral hazard was formulated by insurers in the 1600s, but the phrase itself didn't come into usage until the 1800s. When insurance companies first used it, the phrase had pejorative connotations, with moral hazard being invoked when insuring supposedly dubious characters and also, predictably, certain ethnic and social groups. This is hinted at in the Merriam Webster definition of the phrase: "The possibility of loss to an insurance company arising from the character, habits, or circumstances of the insured."

With time, the usage became more "value-neutral," showing up in banking in the 1920s when deposit insurance was first considered. In the 1960s, economists latched onto the term and began churning out studies in large numbers. These days, the term can be found not just in insurance and banking but wherever risk is off-loaded. A good argument can be made, for example, that moral hazard enabled the mortgage industry to lower its standards because brokers could pass the risk to lenders, lenders to banks, banks to investors. No one thought themselves responsible. No one had any skin in the game.

In insurance and economics, the term will lead you into statistical mazes. In banking, it's become a governing principle. Do we let errant bankers continue in business or do we sit back and allow the survival of the fittest, come what may? There are partisans on both sides of the moral-hazard divide, some arguing that ignoring it has brought us to the current sorry pass, the other side saying that it's an antiquated concept that has no place in modern banking. The term is still value-neutral, although our attitude toward the employment of it and toward bankers isn't.

Time and again, argue moral-hazard fundamentalists, both Republican and Democratic administrations have ignored moral hazard and averted financial-sector crises by one means or another, and time and again the only lesson that bankers have learned is that they pay no penalty for bungling. These bailouts have rendered them not just reckless but stupid about risk. As I have my fictional risk manager say: "Where's the incentive *not* to screw up?" The etymologists among moral-hazard fundamentalists point out that the word "hazard" derives from an early form of craps, a gambling game where fortunes are won or lost on the roll of the dice, which they see as only too appropriate for an industry that has become more casino-like with every passing year.

The fall-out when moral hazard is ignored was made plain recently by Roger Lowenstein in a *New York Times* article marking the tenth anniversary of the Long Term Capital Management meltdown. Like the interviewer in the skit, Lowenstein, author of the highly readable *When Genius Failed: The Rise and Fall of Long-Term Capital Management*, lamented that no one learned anything from that episode, which was, in his words, "a small dress rehearsal" for the chaos now enveloping us. The lessons have become all too familiar: the danger of unregulated derivatives, the perils of excessive leverage, and the fallibility of financial models. As investor Warren Buffet – the Sage of Omaha – likes to say, "Beware of geeks bearing formulas."

Opponents would argue that stopping financial contagion is much more critical than heeding moral hazard. Contagion breeds panic, and panic can bring down institutions that have done nothing wrong. They would also say that some bailouts, such as the LTCM one, don't involve taxpayers' money. And it didn't. The government brought bank CEOs into a room and banged their heads together to make them agree to buy LTCM and unwind its positions, just as J.P. Morgan did to end the 1907 financial panic. No harm, no foul.

When LTCM went bust, I was, naively, astonished to see bankers who fervently espoused free markets unwilling to let LTCM go south because they had skin in the game. The hypocrisy was galling. In the LTCM case, a few heads rolled, but top bank executives and boards of directors stayed in place. In this recent round, some CEOs were ousted but walked off with a king's ransom in compensation. The buck never stops. No culpability, no penalty – that's the harm.

The same people who let the government stop them from falling into an abyss violently opposed regulation that might have prevented them from falling into an abyss in the first place. After that first speech, I wrote many others that claimed that bankers could police themselves. As I laboured over the message, I couldn't help but think, what nonsense! There is an obvious human propensity toward deceit, especially when money is involved. I also heard repeatedly that regulators, those poor stumblebums, were ten years behind investment bankers in their thinking. Turtles trying to catch up with racehorses *et cetera*. All they did was hinder financial ingenuity. Appears now the bankers were the stumblebums, albeit ones in custom-tailored suits.

While there is plenty of blame to go around, ignoring moral hazard and rolling back regulation almost certainly have played a large part in bringing about a crisis on a scale that even the most bearish and Henny Penny-ish among us could hardly have imagined. The situation is so out of hand that moral hazard, mooted when the crisis first began and heeded belatedly in the case of Lehman Brothers, has been ditched even as a theoretical principle and replaced by a policy that's best described as print money and throw it wildly, indiscriminately, and see if it sticks, creating layer upon layer of moral hazard.

Whether one is for or against moral hazard, it's been clear for some time that banking couldn't continue in its present form for one reason: computers. They allow such gigantic flows in and out of markets at such breathtaking speed that it's impossible to control risk. We are back to Clay Shirky and "here comes everybody." Markets, which require a degree of order and balance to function, become unmanageable when "here comes everybody." Diverse surprises, yes, few of them good. As well, computers have enabled financial products to proliferate and be leveraged every which way to Sunday. Computers amplify information and rumour, a vital market engine, to thunderous proportions. They turbocharge greed, stupidity and lemming-like behaviour, never in short supply, and the cream – prudence – gets dispersed, pushed to the bottom. A banker friend, who has been involved with the commodity markets his entire life, remarked that to think we can control risk in these circumstances is a besetting and dangerous vanity. A complete rethinking is due.

Be prepared, though, for the banking industry to argue against regulation despite everything that has happened, to blather, po-faced, about the integrity of the free markets. Back in April, Josef Ackermann, head of the Institute of International Finance, which represents the world's largest financial companies, acknowledged that though mistakes had been made, it would be "completely wrong" for authorities to impose greater regulation: "We want to demonstrate that we can do a better job within the industry." Bankers can be, if nothing else, brazen. Confidence in them will be harder to restore than in the markets. As Ogden Nash wrote, "Consider the banker. / He was once a financial anchor." Past tense.

Glenn Thrush, who covers Congress and the presidential campaign for Politico website, writes, "We've all become business reporters. Each day seems like it's a year long. It's like a crossing of wires – we're covering monumental presidential developments with key legislative developments and then there's the monumental business story."

To which I can only shake my head and say, ain't that the truth. Tsunami year! Tsunami election! Tsunami financial crisis! Politics and the economy have become entwined like a rugged, fast-growing species of ivy taking over a building, pulling out bricks, damaging foundations. The two have certainly taken over our brains. It's the end of September, thirty days to the election. What follows is my take on the run-up to the election in an attempt to convey what it felt like in New York City at a time when every day felt like a year and we became slightly crazed from worry but also mesmerised, unable to switch off the cable news stations, obsessively tracking the DOW, VIX, LIBOR spreads, polls in red states. So much at stake.

Every morning around 8.30 a.m., I read Barbara Rockefeller's foreign-exchange newsletter – <rts-forex.com> – because she has clear and often amusing summaries of what's happening in the markets. Here is one of her postings from earlier in the year: "Pundits are now saying the recession will be shallow but long-lasting. Keep in mind the economist's ever-present warning of *pari passu*, meaning 'if everything else remains the same.' But everything else never does remain the same. The world is full of new developments and some of them are one-time shocks that change everything." And there's the rub. There's the trauma.

Sunday, 5 October
On Sunday mornings, the talking heads – the hot-air boys and girls, as James Carville called them before he became one of them – strut their stuff. I usually watch *The Chris Matthews Show*, followed by *Meet the Press*,

now moderated by Tom Brokaw following the death of Tim Russert. Then *The McLaughlin Group*, which gets rowdy, with two liberals and two conservatives clashing, talking over each other. What can I say? It's entertaining.

I took away three things from the talking heads this morning. The first is that the light at the end of the financial tunnel is a train. Second, history tells us whoever is ahead in the polls four weeks out from the election will win. That would be Obama. However, racism might still trump economic distress. And third, we are waiting for a possible terrorist attack. Osama bin Laden would like very much to disrupt the elections. The last is called the October surprise, although some of the talking heads think we've had our surprise: the banking meltdown.

No wonder everyone I know is hyperventilating. The most disturbing news of the day – smallish column in the business pages – is that insurance giant AIG has tootled through nearly all of the US$85-billion bridge loan extended to it by the government only a few weeks back. The plan was for AIG to sell assets to pay back the loan. Now it needs even more money. The worry is that AIG will be so diminished after the sale of profitable units that it won't be able to pay back the loan. And the sell-off hasn't even begun because the credit markets are frozen. Catch-22. Ratings agencies are "startled" by this news. Why isn't everyone else startled? If AIG is plumbing the depths and not finding the bottom, the odds are that many other institutions are doing the same. So, yes, a train.

Meanwhile we've woken up to the fact that Sarah Palin isn't naive but hyper-ambitious. She makes Hillary Clinton look a wimp when it comes to ambition. Now she's whipping up her audiences with appalling accusations, stoking racism and spreading lies worthy of Lee Atwater wherever she goes. "The heels are on, the gloves are off," she declares, smiling widely. "Our opponent ... is someone who sees America it seems as being so imperfect that he's palling around with terrorists who would target their own country." In New York, we bite our nails. How is Palin playing in Middle America, where the working classes have voted against their own economic interests for the last eight years? Will they do it again? That's the constant refrain.

Indeed, fretting about Middle America has been a major pastime for months now. Whatever our party affiliation, New Yorkers are, by and large, socially liberal. We are not the ones being constantly robo-called or bombarded with wall-to-wall campaign ads. Racism is wide and deep in the United States, but economic distress has become deeper and wider, and that can only help Obama. Or so we argue among ourselves.

Obama stays steady, on message. "They'd rather try to tear our campaign down than lift this country up," he tells a crowd in North Carolina. "That's what you do when you're out of touch, out of ideas, and running out of time. So I want all of you to be clear, I'm going to keep on talking about the issues that matter." I hear him described as sure-footed as a mountain goat.

While Palin stokes hateful fires, Joe Biden keeps hammering away at his favourite topic: re-establishing fairness in the United States. I'll give you an example of astonishing unfairness. We hear a lot from McCain and Palin about high-income individuals, tended to like hothouse flowers in the Bush years, being forced to pay more taxes under the Obama administration. Destroying dreams, is how the noxious pair characterise it. They also like to point out that US tax rates on corporations are among the highest among the industrialised nations. They neglect to say that one of the most confounding paradoxes in this country is that while the tax rates on companies and corporations are high, the amount they actually pay is the lowest in the world. In fact, according to the Government Accountability Office, after it looked at tax returns from 1989 to 2008, almost two-thirds of companies in the United States pay no corporate income taxes.

If we take this at face value, it means that two-thirds of American companies fail to turn a profit, which is patently untrue: they are skilfully using a range of tax-avoidance strategies to avoid coughing up a single penny. Corporate profits have soared – 14.1 per cent of the nation's total income in 2006 – while the percentage of these profits paid out in taxes is near its lowest level since the 1930s. To call this a fundamental unfairness is to understate the situation. In a country that has a gigantic budget deficit, decaying infrastructure and shameful health and education systems, it's immoral, even criminal.

Monday, 6 October
Lehman chief Richard Fuld testifies in front of the Congressional Committee on Oversight and Government Reform. I'd gone to Wall Street thinking that bankers, if self-interested, were prudent. Instead, I found the opposite: seat-of-the-pants guys. They could be positively Shakespearian in their juicy hubris and fabulous vainglory. Othello comes to mind when watching Fuld, who seethes as he looks down a nose held so high it's almost perpendicular, broadly hinting that he is the victim of the authorities and market gang-trading while protesting that he lies awake at night wondering what he could have done differently. Methinks he is more likely pondering revenge.

Fuld thinks that the Fed should have pushed for the sale of Lehman, as it did in the case of Bear Stearns, or bailed it out, like Fannie Mae, Freddie Mac and AIG, instead of invoking moral hazard and allowing the firm to go bankrupt. It's become received wisdom that this was a mistake because Lehman's demise was the catalyst that caused the credit markets to freeze. At the time, it's true, the Fed was drawing, if indecisively, a line. It also had counted on institutions lowering risk levels after the Bear Stearns near-collapse six months before, which didn't happen. What's left out of this account is that confidence in the credit markets was already severely eroded – the financial crisis has been going on as long as the elections, running almost in tandem – and Lehman had a black hole at its centre in the form of poisonous derivatives that had a gravitational pull as strong as any in space. Had it been saved, another financial institution would have taken its place: black holes abound.

To loosen up the credit markets, the Fed is now proposing to buy shares in select banks instead of their toxic waste, as first proposed. A better solution, to be sure, given the impossibility of correctly pricing the paper. How the selecting gets done in an industry synonymous with back-door deals and cronyism, well, let's just say it had better be done in the brightest sunshine. All of this, of course, is moral hazard writ in neon, but market confidence comes first.

The DOW drops nearly 800 points, below 10,000 for the first time since October 2004, and then recovers a little. Stocks all over the world follow suit. Iceland's krona resembles a nose-diving gannet. I learn a new word today: capitulation. Apparently that's a true bottom. Instead of going up and down, the DOW hits bottom, stays there and slowly climbs back to a healthy level. Capitulation: when things can't continue, they stop.

The VIX – the stock-market volatility index – goes over 50, the highest it's been since August 1989. Every time the government addresses a problem, we are overtaken by another one. Last Friday, Congress passed the US$700-million bailout bill, which has been given an Orwellian makeover and called TARP, or Troubled Assets Relief Program. We're not bailing out banks, says the government, we're rescuing them. Today, clear signs that European banks are in trouble. Many of them are said to have a leverage level – debt ratio – as high as fifty; Lehman's was thirty-five.

I watched the TARP debate in Congress last week. An eye-opener in regard to the intelligence level of our elected officials. One Republican declared that TARP was a huge cow patty with a little bit of marshmallow in the middle. One of his party colleagues started up about the Bolsheviks and their slogan "peace, land and bread." The present bailout was about "bread and freedom." Lost me. I think he was trying to make a point about the bailout being not just socialist but communist. A Democrat questioned giving US$700 billion to an administration that's been wrong on just about everything. "If you think they will be responsible with the money," she said, "think again."

Small item: A 35-year-old ex-Goldman Sachs banker, Neel Kashkari, the Treasury's assistant secretary for international affairs, will be the interim head of TARP. I am reminded of the fact that when I worked at J.P. Morgan, the average age of employees was twenty-eight years.

Tuesday, 7 October
Following Dick Fuld's turn in front of the oversight committee, ousted AIG CEOs Robert Willumstad and Martin Sullivan take the stage. Before they appear, Eric Dinallo, Superintendent of the New York State Insurance Department, and Lynn Turner, a former chief accountant at the Securities and Exchange Commission (SEC), set out what went wrong with AIG and how it might be fixed. The two men do this brilliantly, exuding Warren Buffett-like decency and common sense. Their most shocking revelation is not about AIG but the SEC, which has been gutted like so many other watchdog agencies in the name of small government. Astoundingly, given the importance of its function, the SEC's Office of Risk Management was cut back to one person. The word on the SEC is that it has gone from watchdog to lapdog, and this explains in part why. Asked if one person could be effective, Turner replies that he was able to turn out the lights at night.

Because it's like shooting fish in a barrel, I won't dwell on the AIG executives, except to note Sullivan's tan, mahogany in colour. Another AIG revelation: Joe Cassano, the head of the company's Financial Products Unit, is still on the payroll. He's being paid US$1 million a month to help AIG unwind his unit's disastrous positions. Back in August of 2007, Cassano said, "It is hard for us, without being flippant, to even see a scenario within any kind of realm of reason that would see us losing one dollar in any of those transactions."

Stephen Colbert coined the word "truthiness." Now Tina Fey in her send-ups of Sarah Palin has coined another: "mavericky." The *New York Times* on 4 October ran an entertaining piece by John Schwartz headed "Who You Callin' a Maverick?" Entertaining enough to post in full:

There's that word again: maverick. In Thursday's vice-presidential debate, Gov. Sarah Palin of Alaska, the Republican candidate, used it to describe herself and her running mate, Senator John McCain, no fewer than six times, at one point calling him "the consummate maverick."

But to those who know the history of the word, applying it to Mr. McCain is a bit of a stretch – and to one Texas family in particular it is even a bit offensive.

"I'm just enraged that McCain calls himself a maverick," said Terrellita Maverick, 82, a San Antonio native who proudly carries the name of a family that has been known for its progressive politics since the 1600s, when an early ancestor in Boston got into trouble with the law over his agitation for the rights of indentured servants.

In the 1800s, Samuel Augustus Maverick went to Texas and became known for not branding his cattle. He was more interested in keeping track of the land he owned than the livestock on it, Ms. Maverick said; unbranded cattle, then, were called "Maverick's." The name came to mean anyone who didn't bear another's brand.

Sam Maverick's grandson, Fontaine Maury Maverick, was a two-term congressman and a mayor of San Antonio who lost his mayoral re-election bid when conservatives labeled him a Communist. He served in the Roosevelt administration on the Smaller War Plants Corporation and is best known for another coinage. He came up with the term "gobbledygook" in frustration at the convoluted language of bureaucrats.

This Maverick's son, Maury Jr., was a firebrand civil libertarian and lawyer who defended draft resisters, atheists and others scorned by society. He served in the Texas Legislature during the McCarthy era and wrote fiery columns for The San Antonio Express-News. His final column, published on Feb. 2, 2003, just after he died at 82, was an attack on the coming war in Iraq.

Terrellita Maverick, sister of Maury Jr., is a member emeritus of the board of the San Antonio chapter of the American Civil Liberties Union of Texas.

Considering the family's long history of association with liberalism and progressive ideals, it should come as no surprise that Ms. Maverick insists that John McCain, who has voted so often with his party, "is in no way a maverick, in uppercase or lowercase."

"It's just incredible – the nerve! – to suggest that he's not part of that Republican herd. Every time we hear it, all my children and I and all my family shrink a little and say, 'Oh, my God, he said it again.'"

"He's a Republican," she said. "He's branded."

Lucy Kellaway, the very funny and delightfully cynical *Financial Times* columnist, reports on management follies. She receives her material over the transom, so to speak, from employees fed up with guff as well as from companies touting their management messages and publicists pushing a steady stream of books on the subject. But with the financial crisis, the stream has dried up. In the past three weeks, she hasn't received "one daft email or daft invitation to attend a management training course based on a study of ancient tribes. No stupid theories, no strategy trees, no new management jargon, no nonsense of any sort. Since I started monitoring these things fifteen years ago I have never known such a scarcity of silliness." She's afraid that the glory days of management bullshit are over.

A dental appointment takes me over to the East Side. In a store window on Madison Avenue, a woman is tending to a mink coat. With a comb, she makes sure the hairs lie exactly right. Bright, guilty world.

The second presidential debate, with its faux town-hall setting, is anticlimactic. Grandpa and Junior. Obama has patience and gravitas, sits still and pays attention whenever McCain speaks. But when Obama speaks McCain wanders the stage like an Ancient Mariner. Or someone who has lost his GPS system, as the comics start saying. I want McCain to ask Obama about Bill Ayers so he can set the record straight. And I want Obama to ask McCain about the Keating Five and his role in the 1987 thrift scandal. And as with the first debate, I want him just once to look down and say to McCain, "Pants on fire!"

The VIX reaches a record high of 59.06 and the level of commentary on CNBC reaches a record low when one of their dishy analysts – the brunette babes hired to mouth market platitudes in the same way that automakers drape bosomy blondes on the hoods of autos – blurts, "Be prepared to lose your lunch."

Wednesday, 8 October
The Federal Reserve, the European Central Bank and other central banks announce rate reductions within seconds of one another. The British prime minister, Gordon Brown, reveals a plan to pump billions of pounds into the country's leading banks. His decisiveness, a relief after President Bush's empty assurances and Treasury Secretary Paulson's shilly-shallying, makes him go from washed-up disappointment to hero overnight. Whenever I think of Bush and Hank Paulson and their lack of leadership, I start humming a Bob Dylan song: *I've been shooting in the dark too long / When something's not right, it's wrong.*

The crisis in United States and European economies has spread to export-dependent developing countries. In Tokyo, the Nikkei 225 index plunges 9.4 per cent; in Hong Kong, the Hang Seng index tumbles 8.2 per cent. In Indonesia, the authorities shut down the stock exchange by late morning because the drop is so precipitous. What's happening is that foreign investors, in particular hedge funds, are dumping everything they can to make up for losses. When the European markets open, the same spooked sell-off continues.

On the *NewsHour with Jim Lehrer* on the PBS television station, reporters from battleground states underscore the problem of race and the polls. "No one can quantify it," says Mackenzie Carpenter at the *Pittsburgh Post-*

Gazette. In the plus column in that state, Democratic registration is at an all-time high, with 94 per cent of eligible voters enrolled.

All the late-night comics — Leno, Letterman, O'Brien — are making whoopee with John McCain's bizarre meandering around the town-hall set of the presidential debate yesterday. But Jon Stewart hits the jackpot. Stewart shows footage of McCain crisscrossing behind Obama and even in front of his opponent as he is speaking, blocking the camera and making the moderator Tom Brokaw peer around him. McCain clasps his hands as he roams, occasionally unclasping them — one of his tics — to hold up a palm. "What are you doing, McCain?" asks an incredulous Stewart. He then tells us that they have isolated the feed from McCain's microphone during his "sojourn" and replays the footage with the soundtrack. With Obama in full throat and the CNN banner at the bottom of the screen reading "Should Healthcare Be Treated as a Commodity?" McCain wanders over to the audience, asking them softly, "What's goin' on over here? How're you folks doing?" Over to the chairs and then, as he makes his way back to the outer reaches, he asks, ever so plaintively, "Has anyone seen my dog? Has anyone seen my little Mr Puddles?" Unclasps his hands, palm up. "Just a little guy. Fits right in your hand. No? Mr Puddles, Mr Puddles, I have snausages …"

Thursday, 9 October
In the biggest share drop since the dark days of 1987, the DOW falls to 8579.19.

The New York Times decides to take a "hard" look at the Greenspan legacy and his position on derivatives. The article, which I have to admit I pounce on with glee, begins by giving the opinions of the three men I think of as the grown-ups of Wall Street. Financier and all-round-good-guy George Soros avoids derivatives created by the pointy-head mathematicians known as quants "because we don't really understand how they work." Felix Rohatyn, the investment banker who saved New York from bankruptcy in the '70s, describes them as "hydrogen bombs."

And Warren Buffett thinks they are "financial weapons of mass destruction, carrying dangers that … are potentially lethal."

On to Greenspan. Flying madly, blindly, in the face of facts, he continues to defend the use of derivatives. The problem is not that the contracts failed, he argued in a Georgetown speech last week, but that people got greedy. A lack of integrity spawned the crisis. No need to regulate the derivatives market, which is now topping US$531 trillion, up from $106 trillion in 2002, because the current crisis will insure a surplus of integrity in the future.

The article brings up the 1999 Senate Banking Committee hearing when Senator Phil Gramm attempted wit by invoking Lincoln and outmoded clothes. Memorably, he also told Greenspan that he "will go down as the greatest chairman in the history of the Federal Reserve Bank." Greenspan gave back the love by telling Gramm, "There is a very fundamental trade-off of what type of economy you wish to have. You can have huge amounts of regulation and I will guarantee nothing will go wrong, but nothing will go right either."

Others weren't so sure. "Aren't you concerned with such a growing concentration of wealth that if one of these huge institutions fails that it will have a horrendous impact on the national and global economy?" asked one senator.

"No, I'm not," Mr Greenspan replied. "I believe that the general growth in large institutions has occurred in the context of an underlying structure of markets in which many of the larger risks are dramatically – and I should say, fully – hedged."

As the economy worsens, Obama is building up a steady lead in the polls. This development causes the talking heads to ask, talent or timing? At McCain rallies, the party faithful are expressing surprise that their candidate could possibly be losing. "And we're all wondering why that Obama is where he's at, how he got here," says one fellow, addressing McCain. "I mean, everybody in this room is stunned that we're in this position." Another says, "I'm mad. I'm really mad. And what's going to surprise you, it's not the economy. It's the socialists taking over our country."

Friday, 10 October
On CNBC an analyst says the stock markets are the tail and credit and money markets are the dog. The tail has lost 2000 points over ten days. This is now referred to as a "cascading crash." The world's leading finance ministers are meeting with Hank Paulson over the weekend. In case they don't come to any agreement and the cascade continues, I decide to beef up my emergency money – the cash I always keep in my sock drawer in case there is a blackout and ATMs don't work. If I'm doing it, so are others. Money under the mattress.

At a rally on Tuesday in Clearwater, Florida, Sarah Palin said Obama was being "less than truthful" about his ties to former Weatherman Bill Ayers. "His own top adviser said they were 'certainly friendly' ... I am just so fearful that this is not a man who sees America the way that you and I see America – as the greatest source for good in this world." This comes one day after Palin's mention of Obama "palling around" with Ayers prompted a true believer to yell, "Kill him!" Also in Clearwater, a racial slur was flung at a black member of the press. Further along the campaign trail that day, someone shouted, "Treason!"

Obama doesn't take the bait, saying at a rally in Chillicothe, Ohio, "They can run misleading ads, they can pursue the politics of anything goes. It will not work. Not this time. I think that folks are looking for something different this time. It's easy to rile up a crowd, nothing's easier than riling up a crowd by stoking anger and division. But that's not what we need right now in the United States. The times are too serious." McCain pipes up, "But I also, my friends, want to address the greatest financial challenge of our lifetime with a positive plan for action."

Cindy McCain, who up until now has looked not only unhappy but heavily medicated – a blonde Morticia – has been energised by her husband's underdog status. She brings up her son, Jimmy, who is serving in

Iraq, at a Pennsylvania rally: "The day that Senator Obama cast a vote not to fund my son when he was serving sent a cold chill through my body, let me tell you." The McCains have often said they didn't want to "drag" Jimmy into the campaign.

Saturday, 11 October
At a rally in Minneapolis, a man tells John McCain he is scared of an Obama presidency. McCain stumbles through his reply, unable to look at the audience: "First of all, I want to be president of the United States and obviously I do not want Senator Obama to be. But I have to tell you, I have to tell you, he is a decent person and a person that you do not have to be scared of as president of the United States." The audience boos their disagreement.

McCain keeps trying to put the evil genie back in the bottle: "The point is, that I will point out [Obama's] record, but I will do it with respect, and I will do it with respect and I want all of you to tell your friends and neighbours the difference between rhetoric and record, but let's do it respectfully."

Elsewhere on the campaign trail, Obama thanks McCain: "I appreciated his reminder that we can disagree while still being respectful of each other."

A McCain campaign ad titled "Dangerous," complete with a B-horror-movie organ-music soundtrack, is playing to wide audiences.

Sunday, 12 October
Georgia Democrat John Lewis, a veteran of the civil-rights movement, says the negative tone of the Republican presidential campaign reminds him of the nasty racist stuff peddled by segregationist Alabama governor George Wallace in the 1960s. McCain reacts by saying that Lewis's remarks are "shocking and beyond the pale." The Obama campaign also distances itself from Lewis's remarks. Not comparable, says a spokesman. The campaign doesn't want to get into race, just concentrate on the economy.

The Obama campaign is bringing in US$7 million dollars a week. Some is spent on television ads and mailers but much of it is devoted to the on-the-ground effort of getting every possible voter to the polls. An army of employees and volunteers is endeavouring to change the electoral map by putting in play states like Indiana, North Carolina and Virginia.

Voter registration, particularly among the young, has ballooned, but that's only half the battle. "We're going to have to make sure they turn out, or we probably won't win," said Obama campaign manager Steve Hildebrand. "They'll get extra waves of mail. They'll get extra phone calls. They will be given a lot of love."

The Obama people aren't knocking randomly on doors. They're using a sophisticated battery of databases along the lines of the ones that the Republicans developed in the last election. Income level, shopping habits, magazine subscriptions, type and make of autos, commuting patterns, voting history in local races – everything that could possibly be relevant is factored in.

"We've been designing and we've been engineering and we've been at the drawing board and we've been tinkering," says Obama, commenting on the get-out-the-vote effort. "Now, it's time to just take it for a drive. Let's see how this baby runs."

"Are they a mile wide and an inch deep?" asks McCain campaign manager Trey Walker. "We'll find out on election day."

Monday, 13 October
Drama! Following Gordon Brown's lead, Hank Paulson changes course and announces that the Treasury will push billions directly into the banks instead of buying troubled assets, as was first proposed when TARP was passed by Congress. He summons the heads of the big banks to Washington to an emergency meeting to tell them that US$250 billion will be made available, to be followed by more as needed. Details of the meeting are sketchy, except that the bank heads, cell phones to their ears, are sighted scuttling to their limos. The DOW surges 936 points, the biggest

one-day rally on stock markets in seventy years. High-five-ing on the floor of the stock market.

Obama calls on Americans to embrace a new "ethic of responsibility": "I won't pretend this will be easy. George Bush has dug a deep hole for us. It's going to take a while for us to dig our way out. We're going to have to set priorities as never before." He gently scolds all Americans for "living beyond their means – from Wall Street to Washington to even some on Main Street."

Tuesday, 14 October
Neel Kashkari says the Treasury Department's "equity injections" will be aimed at "healthy" firms. Who gets to do the deciding? The large number of ex-Goldman Sachs employees involved in the rescue plan has prompted wags to make cracks about "Government Sachs." Conflict of interest, anyone?

And will any of the banking heads face the consequences of bad decisions? So far they have shown zero leadership, zero initiative. In fact, they imply that we should thank them for taking all that money onboard. They're making Bush look good.

In Europe, the bailout money for banks will be around US$1.4 trillion, almost exactly double what the US is ponying up. Yep, it's one-upmanship, a pissing competition between the boys. Just what we need with the world going to hell in a hand-basket. With undisguised glee, President Sarkozy has been announcing the death of American-style capitalism: "*Laissez-faire est fini.*" Let's call it casino capitalism – and the Americans weren't the only ones at the craps tables and trying their luck with the one-armed bandits.

Wednesday, 15 October
The last presidential debate is almost too wretched to watch because Obama must remain bland and inoffensive. This is called "sitting on his lead." He can't afford to rip into McCain for fear of being perceived as an

angry black man. He can't even crack a joke. McCain blinks and sneers like a possessed possum, injecting Joe the Uncertified Plumber into the nation's discourse for several news-cycles.

Along with his comment about small-town Americans being "bitter," Obama must surely regret telling Joe that wealth should be spread around. It immediately ignited an unstoppable conflagration of accusations that he was not just a liberal but – egads! – a socialist, unlike the Fed, which is merely "rescuing" banks. These are his only two missteps in eighteen months. Republicans declare it the best debate for McCain; viewers think otherwise, with a CNN poll registering that 70 per cent of viewers found Obama more likeable, 22 per cent, McCain.

Details are coming out about the emergency meeting at the Treasury on Monday with the bank chieftains. Hank Paulson bent over backwards to tell bankers that the idea of giving them mountains of dosh to tide them over hard times was "regrettable" – ideologically incorrect, highly aberrant. He also told them they had no option but to sign the one-page agreement: "The alternative of leaving businesses and consumers without access to financing is totally unacceptable." Ben Bernanke chimed in with variations on the theme of confidence. You might say the infusion of capital is US$250 billion of free-market humble pie for everyone concerned.

The bankers were genuinely shocked at the ultimatum. Afterwards Paulson said, "I don't think there was any banker in that room who was going to look us in the eye and say they had too much capital." Dick Kovacevich, the chairman of Wells Fargo, apparently thought otherwise, immediately saying that, unlike his New York rivals, his bank did not need a bailout. He also complained about the restrictions on executive compensation because he will receive a big payday – US$43 million, and $140 million in accumulated stock and options – if he steps down when Wells Fargo completes a planned takeover of Wachovia.

Sense returned when Ken Lewis, chairman of Bank of America, which has just acquired once-proud Merrill Lynch, told his colleagues that "we are out of our minds" to make a fuss about executive compensation. That he had to say this is perhaps the most telling detail of all. Between them, the executives in the room received US$231 million in compensation last year.

The stock market drops 733 points as doubts about the Paulson plan spread.

A photograph arrives by email, taken at a demonstration on Wall Street. I send it to my broker at Merrill Lynch, an old-timer who has seen every possible form of banking cock-up over the years. He can't stop laughing. Déjà-vu all over again, to quote Yogi Berra.

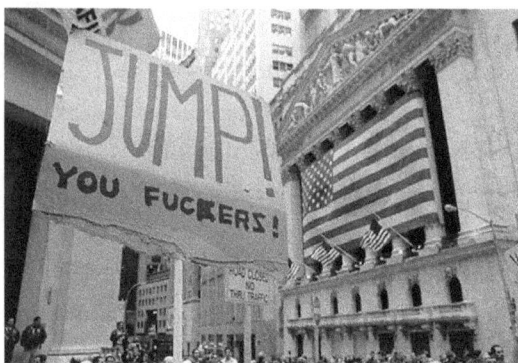

Thursday, 16 October
The VIX reaches its highest point ever: 81.7. I turn off the television and read *The Girl with the Dragon Tattoo*, a mystery by Swedish writer Stieg Larsson. Timely as all hell because it has a financial scandal as part of the plot. The Swedes know a thing or two about financial implosions because they had to nationalise their banks back in 1992 when their housing bubble burst. When the banks had stabilised they were privatised again; taxpayers got their money back.

Friday, 17 October
The commentators on CNBC have adapted to the wild market. No more comments about losing their lunch. When the VIX hit 50, they got

market-sick. Now that the VIX has gone as high as 81.7, they are seasoned sailors, riding the steep drops and equally steep ascents created by hedge funds frantically selling into the market ahead of investors redeeming their money, and others equally frantically buying into the markets to snaffle up "opportunities." Manic Monday, Meltdown Monday, Tsunami Tuesday, Frantic Friday. It's as if market players are stranded on a desert island without food, and they've turned cannibal. The bank bailouts and the temporary suspension of short selling aside, we still have free markets. Darwinian markets. The bad news about the US economy keeps rolling in.

There is no sign that confidence in the banks has been restored. The banks are hoarding the government infusion, keeping it as part of their profit-making structure and capital requirements and not directing it to people who need the money – homeowners, students, small businesses. As former Secretary of Labor Robert Reich succinctly puts it, "This is socialism for the rich, capitalism for the rest of us. The banks have socialized their losses, privatized their profits." David Brooks, one of two conservative columnists at the *New York Times*, has provided many of us with entertainment of sorts this year as he's evaded acknowledging the mistakes of the Bush administration and the McCain campaign. In particular, he's squirmed this way and that in regard to Obama. Until today. "There has never been a moment when, at least in public, he seems gripped by inner turmoil." writes Brooks. "It's not willpower or self-discipline he shows as much as an organized unconscious. Through some deep, bottom-up process, he has developed strategies for equanimity, and now he's become a homeostasis machine."

This leads Brooks to sketch out two scenarios for an Obama presidency. In the first scenario, "[Obama] would be untroubled by self-destructive demons or indiscipline. With that cool manner, he would see reality unfiltered. He could gather – already has gathered – some of the smartest minds in public policy, and, untroubled by intellectual insecurity, he could give them free rein. Though he is young, it is easy to imagine him at the cabinet table, leading a subtle discussion of some long-term problem."

In the second scenario, all too easy for Brooks to imagine, "he is not an island of rationality in a sea of tumult, but simply an island ... Lost in his own nuance, he will be passive and ineffectual. Lack of passion will produce lack of courage. The Obama greatness will give way to the Obama anti-climax ...We can each guess how the story ends. But over the past two years, Obama has clearly worn well with voters. Far from a celebrity fad, he is self-contained, self-controlled and maybe even a little dull."

A homeostasis machine. Dull. Boring. That's the verdict conservatives have latched onto, in the same way that they blame McCain's downward spiral in the polls only on the economy, not on his crotchety behaviour, pandering policies, pick of running mate.

As Brooks was filing his column, Senators McCain and Obama came together last night at the Alfred E. Smith Memorial Foundation Dinner, held at the Waldorf-Astoria in New York. Al Smith was a progressive politician whose ideas foreshadowed the New Deal, and the dinner, which takes the form of an amusing roast in aid of Catholic Charities, has become a tradition, a moment of levity before the grind of the two weeks leading up to the election. It's not just an occasion for the nominees to have some fun – it's also when speechwriters, as confined by campaign necessities as the candidates, can let rip. You might remember that this was the dinner where George W. Bush told the white-tie crowd, "This is an impressive crowd. The haves and the have-mores. Some people call you an elite. I call you my base." Words that he capped with his megawatt smirk.

We all know that McCain has a sense of humour. In fact, he can be downright vulgar. At a Republican fundraiser, he asked the audience why Chelsea Clinton was so ugly. Answer: her mother is Janet Reno. This awful joke was so inappropriate that it made my neurologist speculate as to whether McCain had a disinhibiting dementia. (This doctor isn't the only one diagnosing McCain. More than two thousand physicians placed an ad in the *New York Times* asking McCain to be more forthright about his health.) At the Smith dinner, surrounded by Catholic worthies and seated next to Cardinal Egan, he kept to the straight and narrow, beginning by announcing that he had dismissed his entire team of senior advisers. "All of their positions will now be held by a man named Joe the Plumber," he cracked.

Obama, however, was the candidate who was most obviously relishing being able to relax, to throw off the "dull" mantle and flash his megawatt smile, missing from all the debates: "John McCain is onto something. There was a point in my life when I started palling around with a pretty ugly crowd, I've got to be honest. These guys were serious deadbeats; they were lowlifes; they were unrepentant no-good punks. That's right: I've been a member of the United States Senate."

They poked fun at themselves and each other. McCain made light of his blunder in calling Obama "that one" during the second debate. "He doesn't mind at all," Mr McCain said. "In fact, he even has a pet name for me: George Bush." Obama followed up by telling the crowd that his first name was actually Swahili for "that one."

Obama dispatched Sarah Palin by deadpanning, "I do love the Waldorf-Astoria. You know, I hear that from the doorstep you can see all the way to the Russian Tea Room." But my favourite Obama joke of the evening was when he said, "There is no other crowd in America that I'd rather be palling around with right now. It is often said that I share the politics of Alfred E. Smith and the ears of Alfred E. Newman." Paying homage to two great Americans.

LIBOR rates, an important index of banks' willingness to lend to each other, are contracting. Efforts continue to get a clearing house in place for the US$55 trillion of credit-default swaps to bring transparency to the market – a measure some authorities and thoughtful market participants have been trying to accomplish for several years. Initially intended to be a form of insurance for securities, credit-default swaps devolved at many banks into undisguised gambles. That is, the buyers and sellers of these contracts were neither the lender nor the borrower. As Barbara Rockefeller notes, "It's a big bookie operation like a sports book, and the Fed is annoyed that such frivolity is hanging like a sword over our heads."

Meanwhile, in the *New York Times* Warren Buffett loses some of his lustre for me by opining that people shouldn't feel comfortable putting their money in cash. "They have opted for a terrible long-term asset," he scolds, "one that pays virtually nothing and is certain to depreciate in value … Equities will almost certainly outperform cash over the next decade, probably by a substantial degree. Those investors who cling now to cash are betting they can efficiently time their move away from it later. In waiting for the comfort of good news, they are ignoring Wayne Gretzky's advice: 'I skate to where the puck is going to be, not to where it has been.'" Terrible? Buffett might feel comfortable taking his money out of Treasuries and buying US stocks, but he's also the richest man in the United States. He can afford to win some, lose some. Also, when I worked on Wall Street, Wayne Gretsky skating to the puck was a rah-rah staple of speeches. A line so hoary that it could stand up by itself, so over-used that it has less value than a Lehman CDO.

Saturday, 18 October
I talk with a friend, Desmond, about my assumption that investment bankers had been made stupid by their arrogance. Desmond replies that arrogance *is* stupidity. Long ago, he worked as a bond trader. After a few months on the job, he said to his boss, "These people are really stupid." Hardly the first person to make this observation of bond traders, who occupy the bottom of the Wall Street heap. "Button your lip," said his boss. "If they were smart we wouldn't make any money."

Desmond later sends me an email with some lines from the beginning of Joseph Conrad's *Victory*: "The world of finance is a mysterious world in which, incredible as the fact may appear, evaporation precedes liquidation. First the capital evaporates, and then the company goes into liquidation. These are very unnatural physics …"

The subject of bankers and stupidity was parsed with vigour by hedge-fund manager Andrew Lahde in a letter to his investors, leaked to a wider audience today. He is closing shop – a tremendously lucrative shop that had an 870 per cent gain last year by betting on the subprime mortgage collapse. The letter is worth posting in full:

> Today I write not to gloat. Given the pain that nearly everyone is experiencing, that would be entirely inappropriate. Nor am I writing to make further predictions, as most of my forecasts in previous letters have unfolded or are in the process of unfolding. Instead, I am writing to say goodbye.
>
> Recently, on the front page of Section C of the *Wall Street Journal*, a hedge fund manager who was also closing up shop (a $300 million fund) was quoted as saying, "What I have learned about the hedge fund business is that I hate it." I could not agree more with that statement. I was in this game for the money. The low-hanging fruit, i.e. idiots whose parents paid for prep school, Yale, and then the Harvard MBA, was there for the taking. These people who were (often) truly not worthy of the education they received (or supposedly received) rose to the top of companies such as AIG, Bear Stearns and Lehman Brothers and all levels of our government. All of this behavior supporting the Aristocracy only ended up making it easier for me to find people stupid enough to take the other side of my trades. God bless America.
>
> There are far too many people for me to sincerely thank for my success. However, I do not want to sound like a Hollywood actor accepting an award. The money was reward enough. Furthermore, the endless list of those deserving thanks know who they are.
>
> I will no longer manage money for other people or institutions. I have enough of my own wealth to manage. Some people, who think they have arrived at a reasonable estimate of my net worth, might be surprised that I would call it quits with such a small war

chest. That is fine; I am content with my rewards. Moreover, I will let others try to amass nine, ten or eleven figure net worths. Meanwhile, their lives suck. Appointments back to back, booked solid for the next three months, they look forward to their two week vacation in January during which they will likely be glued to their Blackberries or other such devices. What is the point? They will all be forgotten in fifty years anyway. Steve Balmer, Steven Cohen, and Larry Ellison will all be forgotten. I do not understand the legacy thing. Nearly everyone will be forgotten. Give up on leaving your mark. Throw the Blackberry away and enjoy life.

So this is it. With all due respect, I am dropping out. Please do not expect any type of reply to emails or voicemails within normal time frames or at all. Andy Springer and his company will be handling the dissolution of the fund. And don't worry about my employees, they were always employed by Mr. Springer's company and only one (who has been well-rewarded) will lose his job.

I have no interest in any deals in which anyone would like me to participate. I truly do not have a strong opinion about any market right now, other than to say that things will continue to get worse for some time, probably years. I am content sitting on the sidelines and waiting. After all, sitting and waiting is how we made money from the subprime debacle. I now have time to repair my health, which was destroyed by the stress I layered onto myself over the past two years, as well as my entire life – where I had to compete for spaces in universities and graduate schools, jobs and assets under management – with those who had all the advantages (rich parents) that I did not. May meritocracy be part of a new form of government, which needs to be established.

On the issue of the US Government, I would like to make a modest proposal. First, I point out the obvious flaws, whereby legislation was repeatedly brought forth to Congress over the past eight years, which would have reined in the predatory lending practices of now mostly defunct institutions. These institutions regularly filled the coffers of both parties in return for voting down all of this legislation designed to protect the common citizen. This is an outrage, yet no one seems to know or care about it. Since Thomas Jefferson and Adam Smith passed, I would argue that there has been a dearth of worthy philosophers in this country, at least ones focused on improving government. Capitalism worked for two hundred years, but times change, and systems become corrupt. George Soros, a man of staggering wealth, has stated that he would like to be remembered as a philosopher. My suggestion is that this great man start and sponsor a forum for great minds to come together to create a new system of government that truly represents the common man's interest, while at the same time creating rewards great enough to attract the best and brightest minds to serve in government roles without having to rely on corruption to further their interests or lifestyles. This forum could be similar to the one used to create the operating system, Linux, which competes with Microsoft's near monopoly. I believe there is an answer, but for now the system is clearly broken.

Lastly, while I still have an audience, I would like to bring attention to an alternative food and energy source. You won't see it included in BP's "Feel good. We are working on sustainable solutions" television commercials, nor is it mentioned in ADM's similar commercials. But hemp has been used for at least 5,000 years for cloth and food, as well as just about everything that is produced from petroleum products. Hemp is not marijuana and vice versa. Hemp is the male plant and it grows like a weed, hence the slang term. The original American flag was made of hemp fiber and our Constitution was printed on paper made of hemp. It was used as recently as World War II by the US Government, and then promptly made illegal after the war was won. At a time when rhetoric is flying about becoming more self-sufficient in terms of energy, why is it illegal to grow this plant in this country? Ah, the female. The evil female plant – marijuana. It gets you high, it makes you laugh, it does not produce a hangover. Unlike alcohol, it does not result in bar fights or wife beating. So, why is this innocuous plant illegal? Is it a gateway drug? No, that would be alcohol, which is so heavily advertised in this country. My only conclusion as to why it is illegal is that Corporate America, which owns Congress, would rather sell you Paxil, Zoloft, Xanax and other additive drugs than allow you to grow a plant in your home without some of the profits going into their coffers. This policy is ludicrous. It has surely contributed to our dependency on foreign energy sources. Our policies have other countries literally laughing at our stupidity, most notably Canada, as well as several European nations (both Eastern and Western). You would not know this by paying attention to US media sources though, as they tend not to elaborate on who is laughing at the United States this week. Please people, let's stop the rhetoric and start thinking about how we can truly become self-sufficient.

With that I say good-bye and good luck.

All the best,

Andrew Lahde

Good for you, Mr Andrew Lahde! May you enjoy your spliffs! His letter is a reminder that there is always a counterparty, always someone on the other side of financial bets. Always someone making money by the boatload.

The stores are mostly empty, even the popular big-box chains near me on Broadway. It's as if there's been a citywide anthrax scare. Pottery Barn tried to attract Saturday-morning shoppers by the primitive means of placing a blackboard propped on an easel outside its door to advertise lessons on "how to decorate a table and dress a bed." These activities seem like relics from some long-ago era, like croquet and charades.

Robert Skidelsky, author of a critically acclaimed biography of John Maynard Keynes, notes the boomlet in financial terms: "A whole new vocabulary has spread from board tables to kitchen tables. Superannuated whiz kids planting cabbages to offset their newly straitened means can blame their troubles on collateralized debt obligations, special investment vehicles, credit default swaps. Subprime mortgage holders find themselves censured for a new and virulent disease called toxic debt." I can testify to that. When I was doing publicity for my novel *Moral Hazard* in 2002, I was forever explaining the term. No need for that now.

Keynes thought that professional investment is like "'a game of Snap, of Old Maid, of Musical Chairs,' whose object is to pass on the Old Maid – the toxic debt – to one's neighbor before the music stops," writes Skidelsky. "What makes the game toxic is not greed, which is universal, but uncertainty masquerading as certainty."

Skidelsky reminds us that Keynes's aphorisms, "which seem so apposite today, were for years dismissed with a pitying smile as the product of a primitive state of economic thinking that had been rendered obsolete by powerful desktop computers and Ph.D. math unavailable to economists of Keynes's generation ... We know now that we know very little."

Sunday, 19 October
On *Meet the Press*, General Colin Powell comes out in support of Obama with an eloquence almost equal to Obama's. With the polls showing Obama to have a double-digit lead and his rallies in stout Republican states attracting some of the biggest crowds of the campaign, the talking heads give the election to Obama, with the external-event caveat. An outlier. Conservative commentator Andrew Sullivan thinks that the extraordinary get-out-the-vote campaign, which has swollen the numbers of Democrats registered to vote, means that Obama will win by an even greater margin than the polls say. And, oh yes, Obama's presidency will be the dullest presidency ever.

For their part, the Obama campaign managers are being "superstitious." They're not about to crow. Only two words, they say, are needed: New Hampshire. That's where the pollsters got it wrong in the primaries, giving it to Obama before Hillary Clinton won. When I mention this to Frank, an ex-banker friend who talks regularly with an Obama staffer, he tells me that word has gone out to everyone in the field: "Don't get cocky." The discipline of the campaign on display again.

They are right. No one I know is feeling confident. Everyone I talk to from other countries thinks it will be a shoo-in, but they don't live here. After all, it's only been forty-three years since the *National Voting Act*, when restrictions, such as literacy requirements, that had kept black people from voting, were lifted. And the unexpected has happened all year long. The unexpected need not be external, of course, given the priming of the Far Right by Sarah Palin.

Another prominent Republican has also endorsed Obama: Christopher Buckley, author of the uproarious *Thank You for Smoking* and the son of the dean of conservatives, the late William Buckley, who came to resemble a lizard as he aged, complete with scales and flickering tongue. An elitist, malevolent lizard: Bill Buckley dripped Park Avenue contempt and dismissed opponents with scorching blasts of erudition. For his heresy, Christopher Buckley was immediately removed from the masthead at the *National Review*, the magazine his father founded. "The thought of Sarah Palin as president gives me acid reflux," says Buckley. He adds that his father spent his life trying to separate "the Right from the kooks," which led me to amuse myself by imagining a meeting between Bill Buckley and Sarah Palin. I think Bill would have kept the lascivious drooling in check, unlike Henry Kissinger when he had a tête-à-tête with La Palin.

On *The Daily Show*, Buckley is asked by Jon Stewart whether he will return to the *National Review* fold after the election. He answers by paraphrasing Reagan: "I didn't leave the Republican Party. The Republican Party left me." Buckley hopes that there will be some post-election soul-searching in his party. He pauses – his speech cadences are exactly like his father's – and then adds cheerfully, "There probably won't be."

We are told today that the FBI doesn't have enough agents to investigate criminal financial wrong-doing. Agents were re-assigned to terrorist programs, but the major reason is – surprise, surprise – cutbacks, which "have left the bureau seriously exposed in investigating areas like white-collar crime." The plan is to re-assign several hundred agents, but many inside and outside the Justice Department don't think that will be enough. A shortage of G-men.

Monday, 20 October

Ben Bernanke appears before a congressional committee in the morning and gives the nod to another stimulus package like the one earlier in the year. Along with giving the banks trillions – the amount keeps escalating, we left billions behind last week – the idea is to give taxpayers a couple of hundred bucks each, which we will rush out and spend, boosting the economy. Unlikely given the black holes in household budgets.

Enter economist Anna Schwartz, now ninety-two years old and able to remember the Great Depression, not just study it, as Bernanke has done. Schwartz co-authored with Milton Friedman *A Monetary History of the United States*, which Bernanke acknowledges as the definitive account of how misguided monetary policy turned the stock-market crash of 1929 into the Great Depression.

In an interview in the *Wall Street Journal*, Schwartz argues that the Fed has got it all wrong. According to her, they've gone about it as if there was a shortage of liquidity when the real problem is uncertainty "that the balance sheets of financial firms are credible." The bankers don't trust each other.

Even though the Fed has flooded the credit markets with cash, they remain constipated "because banks don't know who is still solvent and who is not." The problem: derivatives that can't be sold because they can't be valued. Schwartz thought that Hank Paulson's original proposal to buy these assets from the banks was "a step in the right direction," but if the assets were priced at today's levels a number of banks would be insolvent. In shifting from buying bank assets to recapitalising them directly, as Paulson and the Treasury did on Monday, they shifted from trying to save the banking system to saving banks.

Rather, says Schwartz, with welcome bluntness, "firms that made wrong decisions should fail ... Everything works much better when wrong decisions are punished and good decisions make you rich." The trouble is, "that's not the way the world has been going in recent years." The esteemed Anna Schwartz is a moral-hazard fundamentalist.

"It takes real guts to let a large, powerful institution go down, but the alternative – the current credit freeze – is worse," argues Schwartz, who still reports for work at the National Bureau of Economic Research in New York, where she has been employed since 1941. "I think if you have some principles and know what you're doing, the market responds. They see that you have some structure to your actions, that it isn't just ad hoc – you'll do this today but you'll do something different tomorrow." When the authorities drew a line with Lehman Brothers after saving other institutions, they looked erratic, not principled.

She lays the blame for the crisis firmly with Alan Greenspan and his expansive monetary policy: "If you investigate individually the manias that the market has so dubbed over the years, in every case, it was expansive monetary policy that generated the boom in an asset."

The former Fed chairman is busily absolving himself of any responsibility by saying that he had to have an expansive monetary policy or the market would have been "very much displeased." Whatever the market might think, Schwartz contends, the longer the boom, the bigger and more painful the bust: "In general, it's easier for a central bank to be accommodative, to be loose, to be promoting conditions that make everybody feel that things are going well."

Deliciously – if you find such things delicious – Anna Schwartz remembers Ben Bernanke, back when he was the New York Federal Reserve

Board governor, declaring in a speech in honour of Milton Friedman's ninetieth birthday, "I would like to say to Milton and Anna, regarding the Great Depression: you're right, we did it. We're very sorry. But thanks to you, we won't do it again." But they *are* doing it again, Schwartz ruefully acknowledges. Her verdict on the present Fed leadership: "They have not really done their job."

Listen up, boys: "Everything works much better when wrong decisions are punished and good decisions make you rich."

Brooksley Born and Anna Schwartz – my heroes.

Tuesday, 21 October
Credit is supposedly beginning to flow. If you say so. (In New York, whenever someone says something self-evidently wrong and you want to signal polite or amused disagreement, you reply, "If you say so.")

The drumbeat from the McCain campaign is nonsense about the "real" America. Needless to say, New York is not the "real" America. A Republican congresswoman, Michele Bachmann, called last week for an enquiry to uncover which of her colleagues is anti-American. In response, donations have been pouring into her opponent's campaign coffers, US$1 million, more than he's received in the entire year. The congresswoman has denied having said it, transcript to the contrary, making herself even more of a laughing stock. All the same, McCarthy-era language is unsettling.

During the day I compulsively switch from the cable news channel MSNBC, to the financial channel CNBC, to the point that I think that I'm losing it. I'm hardly alone in this behaviour.

At the hairdresser, I hear an Upper East Side woman says to Mr Kim, the Cambodian proprietor, "I'm scared, so scared, that Obama will lose." Mr Kim isn't scared at all. In his view, neither party will do anything for him. He's furious, though, *really* steamed at our billionaire mayor, Michael Bloomberg, who wants to suspend term limits because of the economic crisis and run for four more years. On the whole, Bloomberg has been an effective mayor, but this is "no fair." Slippery slope.

Frank, my ex-banker friend, relates to me a conversation he had with one of New York's top real-estate developers. "If the real-estate slump is a baseball game with nine innings, what inning are we in now?" he asked. The developer replied, "The second inning." Out-and-out gloom and doom from a level-headed, pragmatic businessman.

Across from my apartment, a svelte condo building is rising. I've enjoyed watching it go up because the site is run with extraordinary precision, comforting given the number of cranes that have toppled and killed people in the rush to put up condos. The two cranes for this building are whoppers; they reach higher than my 32nd-floor windows. Grasshoppers out of a science-fiction movie. And it's science fiction I think of when I look out at the city these days, the Hudson River on one side, Central Park on the other, the mass of buildings in between turned into a patchwork by the ever-changing autumn light.

Who will live in the new building if we are only in the second inning? Thousands upon thousands fired on Wall Street, and thousands upon thousands who cater to them, likewise. Rich Russians, Chinese and Indians, once thought to want always to buy apartments here because the US is more stable than their own countries, will stay at home. As well, overseas companies will cancel apartment leases. And then there is the commercial property market. I think not so much of the movie *Blade Runner* as of *Dhalgren*, a novel by Samuel R. Delany in which people eke out a bleak, anarchic existence in a city where an unknown catastrophe has occurred. Delany probably didn't have a financial catastrophe in mind, but the end result could be the same. His novel begins: *to wound the autumnal city. / So howled out for the world to give him a name. / The in-dark answered with wind.*

Wednesday, 22 October
Trying to shake my bomb-shelter state of mind, I take a long walk around the neighbourhood with Sophie. Dogs slow you down, make you pay attention to your world, instead of striding, lost in thought. One block over, in Damrosch Park at Lincoln Center, the Big Apple Circus has set up

its tents for its New York season. A giant banner for Doctor Atomic strains in the wind on the front of the Met Opera. In the next block a huge party tent half a block long is being put in place, complete with multiple a/c units and stairs. Erected for one-night fundraising events, these tents, the money and energy expended in erecting them, have always bothered me. Can't they find a bricks-and-mortar hall in which to eat their filet mignon and write cheques?

It's autumn, already cold. The lobby of my building has filled with leaves, which have somehow gusted by two sets of automatic doors. Sophie is invigorated. She puts her head into the wind, ploughs a path. Soon, though, when the temperature drops to a level known only to her, she will pee and immediately turn tail and beetle inside.

Back in the apartment, I settle down to read Barbara Rockefeller's FX newsletter. Today, she is echoing Andrew Lahde and Anna Schwartz but draws back from out-and-out condemnation. Not just banks but whole countries are being propped up:

> To keep a grip on your perspective of rapidly unfolding events today, keep in mind two words – trust and contraction. The banks have lost trust in one another, their judgment on investments, their ability to judge credit risk of non-banks, and everything else, including whether the sun will rise in the East. As Paulson says (ruefully), we need the banks, even if they are a bunch of second-raters who behave badly. Having worked at banks for twenty years, we affirm that 99 per cent of bankers are second-raters and not people you would invite to dinner at your house. That they have lost trust in one another is in large measure what the psychologists call projection – they know they are second-rate and think the others must be, too. You can't force trust (any more than you can enforce morality) and therefore we have to wait for hysteria to die down under the firm hand of the Treasury and Fed. Nobody likes having government involved, but honestly, it does seem justifiable now.

> Think of the Treasury and Fed as responsible adult Girl Scout leaders
> taking care of 11-year-olds in the woods. No, that's not a monster,
> just an owl and owls do live in the woods, girls.

If you say so, Barbara.

The market tanks again. The VIX is back in the seventies. The system really is cannibalising itself.

Thursday, 23 October
In the two weeks before the US presidential elections, the percentage difference in the polls always narrows. In congressional races between black and white candidates, it *really* narrows. How does that happen? Perhaps because of mailers such as the one the Republican National Committee has put out. On the front of the mailer: "Terrorists don't care who they hurt." Inside: "Obama: Not who you think he is" and the usual guff about his past "associates." Vile, viler, vilest.

Joe Sixpack and Jane Winebox are learning that Sarah Palin has spent US$150,000 on clothes to kit out her and her family for the campaign trail at posh department stores like Neiman Marcus and Saks Fifth Avenue. Comforting earth tones for the family, challenging red patent-leather stilettos for Sarah. Naughty Monkey no longer good enough for her? Freebies are an Alaskan tradition: witness the trial of long-time Alaskan power-broker Senator Ted Stevens, who claims that he was only storing the furniture and exercise equipment given to him by contractors and donors. In New York's bright, guilty world, a $150,000 budget for clothes – on the paltry side. The campaign will donate the clothes to charity after 4 November. If they say so.

AIG is freezing ex-CEO Martin Sullivan's US$19-million severance package, along with approximately $600 million in bonus money for other executives. That's Martin Sullivan of the mahogany complexion. Only freezing it, mind you, and the directors only took the measure because Andrew Cuomo, the state attorney-general, leaned on them. Actually, he threatened the company with legal action, calling the proposed severance "a fraudulent conveyance." The Fed has attached no strings to the US$122.8-billion credit line extended to AIG, which has now drawn $82.9 billion of that sum, all of it to back their side of the credit-default swaps made by the Financial Products Unit. That unit is no longer in existence, assures the new CEO, Edward Liddy, brought in by the Fed. AIG is out of the cold dogshit line of business. Good to hear it!

I check out the huge party tent. Because the tent is on raised land, six sets of stairs have been installed on the street side. Dry-cleaning racks filled with masses of purple and khaki jackets for the waiting staff stand on the pavement. Next to the tent, a large banner advertising the Baron Funds. An investor conference. I hope Baron Funds is better at judging market timing than it is conference timing. Baron Funds specialises in closed-end funds: limited investors, can't get your money back until the fund is liquidated. So how are they doing in the current market? I found this in the *Washington Post*: "A glimpse at the yields of some closed-end bond funds will make your jaw drop. Some of the figures, which are based on the previous 12 months' distributions, top 50 per cent. Throw in the fact that the shares of many of these funds sell for well below the value of the funds' underlying assets, and there seems to be an abundance of screaming buys. Screaming is the operative word here – as in riding that crack-fueled, could-jump-the-tracks-anytime roller coaster." Translation: if you have plenty of money, jump into a fund that has closed-end funds, but be prepared for a heart-in-mouth ride.

At a congressional hearing today, Alan Greenspan, a.k.a the Oracle, expressed "shocked disbelief" at the credit crisis and said he was "partially" responsible because he did not advocate regulation of derivatives. In his usual orotund speaking manner, he confessed to finding a flaw in his ideology: he'd trusted banks to have a stake in their own survival, to be "self-interested" in serving their shareholders. Anyone who has been anywhere near bankers knows that the behaviour of many of them is indeed dictated by self-interest: "I'll be long gone when the shit hits the fan." Greenspan's partial apology, even one through gritted teeth, is better than none at all. Those of us who've always thought Greenspan an enabling ass can take no pleasure in his *mea culpa*, given the havoc he's wrought.

Greenspan qualified his apology by saying that bad data had been fed into the financial models. Bad data? The long-known flaw in computer modelling is that it can only look backward, not forward, because such modelling can't take into account the unpredictability of human behaviour. Emotion – a critical market engine. The topper of Greenspan's testimony: he *still* doesn't think much regulation will be required because the activity of the banks will be "restrained" for some time because of the fall-out from the credit crisis.

Laissez-faire-ists – always finding an angle. My favourite excuse currently coming from bankers is that regulations are too complex for them to follow. First, they hid behind the complexity of structured finance. Greenspan himself claimed that the dot-com and housing bubbles were too complex for him to understand. Banking CEOs followed suit: derivatives were too complex for them to understand. The math certainly can be incredibly complex, but the principles are easy to understand. And if a unit in a bank is minting money, it behoves a CEO and his board to take a gander, figure out how the money is being made, the risk involved, not throw up their hands and say, "Too complex for us!" Whenever bankers use complexity to fend off inquiry, shoot 'em.

Asked on PBS's *NewsHour with Jim Lehrer* whether Greenspan's legacy was affected, Alice Rivlin, respected economist and a former governor at the Fed, graciously said she had enjoyed working with him and thought he was extremely smart but, alack, driven by ideology. That would be Ayn Rand free-market ideology. As a result, Rivlin continued, "he stood in the way of modernising financial regulation," which just about sums up the Oracle's legacy.

One of my best pals, Sue, calls. She can't tear herself away from MSNBC either. She's hooked on the *Huffington Post*. "I'm all over it," she says. I tell her about the *New York Observer's* headline: "The World Serious. New York Is Plowing Its Anxiety Into The Nail-Biter That Has Replaced October Baseball." To relieve our nail-biting, she's bought tickets to a performance by Don Rickles, one of the great "insult" comics. Eighty-two years old – overweight, unsteady on his pins, pigeon walk – he's had a long career because he follows his insults – everyone gets zapped, regardless of gender, sexual orientation and ethnicity, risky when he started – with a sweet, disarming smile. He was a member of Frank Sinatra's Rat Pack. One joke involves Rickles at the Fontainebleau Hotel in Miami Beach, nineteen years old, never been with a girl, so Frank fixes him up with a cocktail waitress, Jennifer, who has blonde hair and a gap between her teeth. Whenever they make love, she whistles. He doesn't know whether he is shtupping her or making tea. That was one of the cleaner jokes.

The audience knows his act back to front. They get on their feet to salute him right through the performance. Those up front reach to touch his hand. Respect bordering on adoration for Borscht-Belt comedy and Rickles in particular. We laugh until we are gasping. I walk home through a world that isn't guilty but definitely bright. Times Square is packed, as are the hotel restaurants and coffee shops. Concertgoers flood out, waves of them, from the various Lincoln Center venues. I could pretend that a worldwide depression isn't imminent. Good-case scenario, it will last two years. Bad-case, twenty years.

Before I leave for the theatre, I watch an interview with McCain and Palin on national television. McCain says that Obama wasn't palling around with terrorists, but "let me tell voters what Bill Ayers and the Weathermen did back in the '60s."

Friday, 24 October
When I worked at J.P. Morgan, I had an office near the top of the building – the 46th floor – with stupendous views of the entire city and both the Hudson and East rivers and their bridges. I could watch the antlike stream of traffic coursing across the Brooklyn Bridge and along the FDR Drive,

tugboats pushing barges in the swift-flowing tidal currents, storms enveloping Midtown Manhattan's skyscrapers. When my boss attempted to remove me from my eyrie, I came close to having a genuine tantrum. All but threw myself on the floor and banged my fists and wailed. The view made the job bearable.

I also had a close-up view of the AIG building across the street. A tower built in the '20s, it featured an executive dining room on its top floor with the kind of art-deco details that make architectural historians salivate. Above the dining room the building ascended in stepped levels that were topped by a mast that was studded with light bulbs. Twice a year, a workman changed those bulbs. He was equipped only with a ladder, a safety harness and a bucket filled with bulbs. Even people who didn't suffer from vertigo had to sit down when they watched this fellow at work fifty storeys above the street. That man and his bucket of bulbs came to mind when Bear Stearns was bailed out, followed by Fannie and Freddie, and then AIG itself. A metaphor for risk – how basic it is. And for regulation – the safety harness.

I now live up high. Thirty-second floor. A number of times every day I get in an elevator that takes me down to the lobby, up to my floor. I never think of the yawning blackness underneath the cab of the elevator or the possibility of malfunction. If I did, I couldn't live here; I've severed myself from the reality of a cab hurtling up and down a void. I enter what amounts to a small room, push a button, and arrive where I want to go. Occasionally when it's very windy, the doors won't close, so you have to push them to meet. The elevators are subject to mandatory inspections, but now and again they make weird thumping and grinding noises, which we report to the front desk, and the repair people are summoned.

In the same way, traders – and their bonuses – have been severed from reality. The numbers exist on a screen. Stocks and bonds used to be real – they'd arrive in trucks and be stored in enormous vaults. These "assets" could be seen and touched. It's said that bankers deal in intangibles:

computers increase the level of intangibility while at the same time legit-imising it. And sitting at a terminal day in, day out, the yawning black space of bad trades somewhere out in the ether – why dwell on it? If they did, traders probably couldn't do the job; they'd be paralysed with fear. You might say that they are in denial about risk – denial that seeps through the entire industry. Unfortunately, the numbers on computers don't make ominous noises, and even if they did, the SEC wouldn't have shown up.

Computers allow traders and their institutions to de-emphasise the tra-ditional nuts-and-bolts side of banking. If anything, though, despite the sophisticated models constructed by quants, the activities of traders have come to resemble those that go on in bucket shops or boiler rooms, dis-reputable establishments that are deemed criminal because they sell secu-rities based on an asset they don't own and don't book the sales through an exchange. Sounds exactly the same as over-the-counter derivatives to me, but what would I know? I'm just a gal in a 32nd-floor apartment going bonkers watching MSNBC and CNBC.

The city council has voted to allow Mike Bloomberg to run for a third term. The *New York Post* puts him on the cover crowned with laurels like a Roman emperor. Asked to comment, Bloomberg admits to thinking, "Oh my goodness. I hope I know what I'm doing."

Obama is visiting his sick grandmother in Hawaii. Knowing no shame, the Republican National Committee is stoking rumours that he is going there to pay off a mistress. Sarah Palin tries to wriggle out of her mistakes, blaming the press, whom she sees as ganging up on her: "If those things were true, I wouldn't like me either."

The Fed is slowly leaking which regional banks will be shored up, which will be allowed to go under. I will refrain from saying anything about moral hazard, layers thereof. We are also discovering that insurance companies across the US are in as bad a shape as the banks. The market swoons, gets up, swoons again. The VIX reaches 90. LIBOR widens.

Saturday, 25 October

Obama's lead slips in the Reuters/C-SPAN/Zog poll from ten points to nine. It's a sure bet that on hearing that, people all over the United States are jumping onto the internet and donating more money to the campaign. I did. Some friends are manning Obama phone banks set up in apartments throughout New York City, others are going house to house out in the battleground states. A lawyer friend is joining the army of volunteer attorneys that will station themselves at polling booths throughout the nation on voting day.

Sunday, 26 October

Last night I went to bed worrying that I'm too obsessed with finance and the ludicrous statements and proposals coming from Washington and just about everywhere else. Enough with the finance, more with the politics. This morning I wake up to find Gretchen Morgenson, one of the *New York Times'* best and most fair-minded business writers, along with Joe Nocera and Floyd Norris, beginning her column with "My hypocrisy meter conked out last week." Apart from the fact that mine conked out ten years ago, I'm glad to know that I was not the only one watching the congressional hearings into the meltdown with disbelief. A bumper crop of bilge.

A good friend, Mary Ann, a retired lawyer and now president of an influential New York City historical preservation society, calls to tell me the time and place for the weekend breakfast down in Greenwich Village that I've been attending through the year. Her husband, Frank, the former J.P. Morgan banker, is also a participant in the group, dubbed the "Parliament" because the purpose of the breakfast is to discuss politics and now, of necessity, finance. The two of them, along with Dubi, a travel agent with an Israeli firm, and Ruth, a long-time Village resident in her eighties and an education expert, form the core of the gathering.

Other friends attend from time to time, along with visitors from out of town, who are sometimes surprised at the vigour of the debate. This breakfast is where we can vent emotions and share information accumulated in the past week, try out theories and generally seek solace. Also, if I have questions about past political eras, these are the people I ask. During the primaries, everyone took different stances on Clinton and Obama – to be expected, we are Democrats – and discussions were Vesuvian. Now we are all holding our breaths until 4 November.

Mary Ann has signed up for one of the many phone banks that have sprung up around the city – groups who gather in apartments with their cell phones, given scripts and phone numbers, and go at it – and she says the experience has been delightful. Her first round of phoning was to the battleground state of North Carolina, and people responded with Southern courtesy. One elderly gentleman told her, "Martin Luther King marched so Obama could run. Obama is running so our children can fly." (I've received one phone call, from a young woman who told me about Congresswoman Michele Bachmann's McCarthyist statements as a way of soliciting a donation; she stumbled badly over all the names, so I ended up giving her a pep talk and thanked her for volunteering.)

Mary Ann also tells me that one of her close friends, a famous UK journalist who has been touring the country, says there will be dancing in the streets all over the world come 5 November. "Hold that thought," says Mary Ann. Better than holding my breath, but I dismiss the optimism as coming from a Brit who doesn't understand race in this country. Because I come from an Australian farming background, I'm more pragmatist than pessimist, although if asked whether a glass is half full or half empty, I will answer, "What glass?"

Prompted by my account of the Don Rickles concert, Ruth tells me an old Jackie Mason joke: "My father was wiped out in the Depression. A stockbroker jumped from a window and flattened his pushcart." And I share with her a piece I've just read in the latest *New York Review of Books* by Mark Danner about an Obama rally in north-west Philadelphia in Pennsylvania, another battleground state. It speaks to our constant anxiety about Middle America. Danner writes about atmosphere, crowd reaction, the give-and-take between candidate and audience, all the things impossible to gauge in New York, where we just get lumpy, unsatisfying soundbites. Here's Danner on one of Obama's speeches to a largely black audience. *Beautiful* writing, in short supply. Danner is criticising the professionals – bloviators and strategists – for whom the rallies serve only as fodder for their "battle of the bites":

> Everything else they [the professionals] would never see. It existed only for the several thousand cheering people in Vernon Park on that bright morning in Germantown. They would never see, for instance, Obama's riff on sweet potato pie. It came as he told a story about his campaigning the other day in a "little town in Ohio, with the governor there" and how he and the governor suddenly felt hungry and "decided we'd stop right there and get some pie." Now all of this led to a quite perfect little gem of a story – the employees wanted to take a picture with Obama, not least because, as they told him, their boss was a die-hard Republican and "they wanted to tweak him a little with that picture." All this was heading toward a perfectly shaped conclusion, where the owner showed up personally with the pie for candidate and governor and Obama looked at the pie and looked at the die-hard Republican owner and "then I said to him" – perfect, perfectly elongated pause – "How's business?" This brought on great gales of laughter from the crowd. For the point had already been precisely made: even if you are a die-hard Republican and you are thinking of your self-interest, how can you vote Republican this year? "If you beat your head against the wall," said Obama, to a blizzard of "oh yeahs!" and "you got that rights!" from the crowd, "and it hurts and hurts, how can you keep doing it?" Those two words – "How's business?" – that casual greeting thrown at the Republican diner owner that showed that there simply could be no other choice this year – that showed the case was proved, wrapped up, unassailable …

And yet what struck me in this perfect little model of political art was a tiny riff inserted into the tiny story, brought on by a shout from the crowd. When Obama launched into his story with "Because I love pie," a woman in the crowd shouted back, "I'll make you pie, baby!" and to the general hooting laughter the candidate returned, "Oh yeah, you're gonna make me pie?" Then, after a beat, amid even more raucous laughter, and several other female voices shouting out invitations, "You gonna make me sweet potato pie?" More shouts and laughter. "All of you gonna make me pie?"

"Well you know I love sweet potato pie. And I think what we're going to have to do here" – and the laughter and the shouting rose and his voice rose above it – "what we're going to have to do is have a sweet potato pie contest … That's right. And in this contest, I'm gonna be the judge." The laughter rose and you could hear not only the women but the deep laughter of the men taking delight in the double entendre that was not only about sex, about that pie that that lanky confident smiling young man knew how to eat and enjoy and judge, but even more now, amazingly, as people came one by one to recognize, about something else. To those people gathered in Vernon Park that bright sundrenched morning, an even more titillating and more pleasurable double entendre, for it was most clearly about something they'd never had but hoped and dreamed of having and now had begun to believe they were within the shortest of short distances of finally tasting. "Because you all know," said the candidate, "that I know sweet potato pie."

Monday, 27 October
Everyone is despairing about the dive in their 401(k) pension plans, which are invested in stocks and bonds. They are also, even the agnostics and atheists, thanking God that Bush failed in his effort to privatise Social Security, which was going to be the crowning achievement of his second

term. Now news is coming out that many of the public pension funds for state and city employees are going broke because fund managers succumbed to the siren call of the high returns offered by structured products and hedge funds. *Unregulated* structured products and hedge funds. All of which was predicted. The dangers inherent in markets – they go down as well as up – and hedge funds – one word: Icarus – were as obvious as dog's balls to anyone with an iota of common sense. But employees were pushed into the plans by companies and corporations who wanted to offload their pension-plan responsibilities.

Indulge me one last time and let me return to my speech-writing days. Along with the advantages of structured finance and the ability of banks to police themselves, two subjects on which I repeatedly had to hammer were the promise of 401(k) plans and the repeal of the *Glass-Steagall Act*. Known as defined-contribution plans, 401(k)s were just beginning to be touted by the banks when I started the job; we used to joke that they sounded like a breakfast cereal. The idea was that employees should be in charge of their destinies and be able to invest their pension money in the markets, which would gain more in value in the long run, or so the banks declared, producing any number of charts to prove their point, over stuffy defined-benefit plans, which grew on compound interest. The advantage to the banks: a Victoria Falls quantity of money spilling into their coffers. Apart from having a fondness for the "sparkling enfilade of compound interest," as James Buchan described it in *Frozen Desire: The Meaning of Money*, I also remember attending a press conference on 401(k)s and wondering what happened if you retired when the stock market was down? What if you retired in a recession or, heaven forbid, a depression? By the end of the decade, common-sense questions such as these were moot because 401(k)s became ubiquitous across the US. Millions are now finding out how poisonous they can be.

Common sense also made me be doubtful about the repeal of *Glass-Steagall*, which was passed in 1933 after the Great Depression to wall off the various areas of banking and insurance from each other so that contagion wouldn't spread. If investment bankers made a mistake, depositors at commercial banks wouldn't be affected; if retail bankers made a mistake, insurance companies would still be solid. The Act was regarded as a fusty relic – a young person's clothes unsuitable for an adult *et cetera* – that might allow foreign competitors who had no such restrictions to overtake US banks. The walls also prevented banks from growing into "convenient" one-stop financial behemoths. As I wrote those speeches – again, my knowledge was sketchy – I had the heretical thought that maybe those walls might have been put in place for reasons that still held: contagion and conflict of interest. In 1999, the banking lobby prevailed and Bill Clinton signed the *Gramm-Leach-Bliley Act*. No trumpet blasts as the walls came down; just a loud purring from satisfied bankers.

Tuesday, 28 October
Felix Rohatyn, Jeffrey Sachs and Nouriel Roubini appear at the New York Public Library in a forum moderated by PBS's Charlie Rose. Title: "Can the Economy Be Saved?" I was on my computer when the email announcement of the forum, hurriedly convened, came through and I pounced on two tickets – the event sold out in minutes. People are hungry to understand what's happening.

Each participant on the panel has a different role. Felix Rohatyn represents common sense. He says that we need to teach Americans the difference between investing and spending. He's referring to Republicans calling opponents "tax-and-spend Democrats," and the kind of investing he's talking about is in infrastructure, which will pay dividends in increased productivity. Government isn't spending on a bridge, it's investing in one.

Economist Nouriel Roubini, ubiquitous in the media because he was one of the first to warn against the dangers of Greenspan's easy-money, bubble-promoting policies, represents the dismal science, economics. He is a model of dismalness, with an unending stream of dire predictions underscored by a slumped posture and a grim unchanging facial expression. He speaks in a monotone, with no pauses between sentences. Wreathed in black clouds but also right on just about everything.

Jeffrey Sachs, director of the Earth Institute and an adviser to UN Secretary-General Ban Ki-moon, represents the globe. He points out that the rich governments have put a cordon around their financial institutions and neglected the repercussions for the developing world. He strikes a rare note of optimism when he talks about the students at Columbia, where he teaches. They're fed up. And they think that radical change is not just necessary but possible.

All of them, including moderator Charlie Rose, agree that an inspiring president along the lines of Franklin Delano Roosevelt will make a huge difference even if economic conditions remain difficult. We are in the middle of the Great Panic not just because of the banks but also because of the yawning leadership void in Washington.

It is Sachs who points out the elephant in the room: the American attitude toward taxation. Not allergic – homicidal. In regard to taxes, the nation is in a permanent state of personal and political denial. For the last three decades, beginning with Reagan, the US has lived beyond its means because it has the lowest tax-collection rate in the developed world. And in that time, the education and health systems, along with critical infrastructure, have rotted. An example: the US is continuing to fall behind in the number of students graduating from high school. Once upon a time Americans had the highest rate; now they are thirteenth, behind South Korea, the Czech Republic and Slovenia. The US has become the only industrialised country where children are less likely to graduate from high school than their parents. If the Great Panic turns into the Great Pruning, Americans might be shocked out of their taxation denial, but I wouldn't count on it; it might mean that they will hold onto their dimes and quarters more tightly than ever before. (Audio for the forum can be heard at <www.nypl.org>.)

While waiting for the event to begin, I read an email from Sue. She stood in line in sour weather to attend a taping of *The Colbert Report*, the program that follows Jon Stewart's *Daily Show*. Sue thinks Stephen Colbert, who plays a Fox News screaming head, is a national treasure. She emails me his best joke at the taping, which sends up the "Obama is an anti-American socialist" drumbeat coming from the Republican camp: "Clearly the McCain campaign is targeting their most important voter: Joe the McCarthy."

Wednesday, 29 October
This morning I stay in bed and watch *House*, *The Mentalist*, *Without a Trace* and *The Shield* before I feel ready to face the world. One credit-default swap too many. I'm not the only one suffering from overload. Here's Barbara Rockefeller on the mood of the markets:

> A droll *Market News* commentator gives us a clue to the prevailing reversal psychology – traders in every market are totally exhausted from endless crisis. "Deleveraging. Balance sheet issues. Hedge fund redemptions. Funding constraints. Margin calls. Month-end. Year-end. Flight-to-quality. Forced liquidations. No risk appetite. Yen-carry unwinds. Is this getting boring or what?" This captures a mood of despair that has become merely boring, so that rising equities seem to be a welcome relief and the only feel-good factor around in a long time. But rising equities are a snare and a delusion. We can understand traders needing relief, but let's be realistic – gloom and doom is here to stay.

Not entirely. The Knicks play the first game of the season under their new coach, Mike D'Antoni. No one dared hope because the team is stuffed with expensive players that can't yet be traded. AND THEY WON! Excuse the *Archy and Mehitabel* lapse into capital letters, but this victory truly warrants it. Jubilation in Madison Square Garden. The "new-look run-and-gun" Knicks made better viewing than the half-hour campaign commercial that Obama ran on all the major network television stations. An infomercial, a genre that is the definition of inauthenticity, but it's a smash hit, gaining 33.55 million viewers, more than the finale of *American Idol* and the last game of the baseball season.

Thursday, 30 October
You would think that there would be no competition between Obama's youth and intelligence and McCain's old-man bumbling and his pitiful hoisting of the underdog flag. As well, according to polls, stark numbers of Americans are finding Sarah Palin to be unfit for the role of veep. But you would be underestimating the American obsession with taxes, now taking centre stage in the last days of the campaign.

You might find the rhetoric on the subject at the McCain–Palin rallies to be Monty-Pythonesque, but plenty of people don't. Last Saturday Palin proclaimed, "When Obama becomes president, what you thought was yours will really start belonging to somebody else. Everyone else. If you thought your property, inventory, investments, were yours – they would collectively belong to everyone."

Joe Biden had an hilarious exchange on the theme with a news announcer named Barbara West from a television channel in Orlando, Florida.

West: "Senator Biden, you may recognise this famous quote. 'From each according to his abilities, to each according to his needs.' That's from Karl Marx. How is Senator Obama not being a Marxist if he intends to spread the wealth around?"

Biden: "Are you joking?"

Hilarious, yes, but the polling gap between Obama and McCain is narrowing, as history indicated it would. Obama might be in the lead, but the McCain campaign's constant refrain about his opponent raising taxes and spreading the wealth is working. In a *New York Times*/CBS poll, 47 per cent of voters say McCain would not raise taxes on people like them, up from just 38 per cent who said so two weeks ago.

As well, the stock market has been more or less steady in the last few days, and that's enough for many to assume everything will be hunky-dory and start listening to balderdash about taxes. Not in New York, however, where the mood is funereal. The Wall Street lay-offs are huge, and no one except brokers peddling stocks thinks the rise in the DOW is permanent. The various parts of the financial markets are rising and falling and going sideways in patterns that defy sense, logic and history. As Nouriel Roubini has been at pains to point out, a "serious disconnect."

Cold water is again dumped on the nation in the form of a report saying that consumer spending is the lowest it's been in nearly thirty years, with business spending not far behind. We're officially in a recession. The DOW doesn't move much – the disconnect – but this dire economic news has a silver lining in that it can only help Obama. Nothing like a recession to focus the minds of voters.

Bill Clinton, who has been a no-show since the convention, has come out of his funk and joined Obama on the trail. Clinton is telling crowds that Obama is "America's future" and Obama is responding by calling Bill "a political genius." Obama knows how to stroke an ego: "When you listen to Bill Clinton, you are reminded of what it's like to have a president who's passionate, who's smart … who has energy, who has vision. You start getting nostalgic about 22 million new jobs and a budget surplus and an economy that's working for everyone."

Friday, 31 October
My political analysis: Obama is brilliant. Joe Biden will make a perfectly good spare. Mavericky McCain has sold his soul to the Far Right. Sarah Palin is a whack job. If the McCain–Palin ticket comes out on top, heaven help us.

I realise that I haven't commented much on Joe Biden. While he's on the side of the angels and has a wicked sense of fun, he's also a Chatty Cathy. The poor fellow has been firmly muzzled by the lockstep Obama campaign because of his gaffes, such as blurting that Hillary would have made a better veep nominee. His worst mistake was saying that the new president is going to be tested by an international incident sooner rather than later. Absolutely true, but the comment placed Obama's lack of experience front and centre. If the Democratic ticket wins, expect Biden to be a source of wisdom, wisecracks and the occasional blooper.

Having delivered those insights, I leave my computer and go down to the Village in search of further hilarity: drag queens dressed as Sarah Palin in the annual Halloween Parade. Nothing like trannies to provide a distraction from thinking about the American purblindness about taxation and the probability of political hanky-panky and malfunctioning voting machines next Tuesday.

On the way, I find the lobby in my building filled with four-year-old princesses and Spidermen stuffing themselves with candy. At the newsagent, the cashier is the Monster Bride, whoever that is, and she looks pretty good. On the subway, Siegfried and Roy with a lion. The parade itself is miles upon miles of New Yorkers of every age, shape and size indulging in fabulous silliness. Some of it is political – yes, trannies as Sarah Palin, a couple as Obama and McCain, both wearing boxing gloves, a fellow as a red-white-and-blue, bullet-shaped Patriot pill holding a banner saying "Under the Influence" – but most are in traditional Halloween garb. Ghosts, witches, ghouls, goblins, skeletons, zombies. My favourite is a group of twenty fellows dressed up as Richard Simmons, dancing to a frantic disco beat.

Further reports are confirming that the tax issue is giving McCain "traction." It's solidifying his base and attracting swing voters. He calls yet again for a lowering of the corporate tax rate so that companies will stay in the US and not decamp to countries where wages are low. Obama doesn't shine a light on evasion of taxes by corporations – too explosive an issue. Instead, he says that Detroit should be saved but restructured. That's called playing it safe.

Whoa! Forget McCain's traction on taxes. Polls are coming at us like meteors. A new one finds that Obama is an average of 6 per cent ahead in most states and has a lead in enough battleground states to get the 270 Electoral College votes he needs for a victory. Maybe the nation is realising that taxes are useful after all; they provide such things as essential services. Could we be about to embrace the idea of an activist government, one that will need a healthy tax base? Oh frabjous day!

An aside: the other thing you need to know about Americans, along with their obsession with taxes, is their love of statistics. Baseball is not about a bat and ball; it's about numbers endlessly sliced and diced, finagled and finessed. Hence the enthusiasm for political polls. Pundits are forever saying that the Electoral College should be abolished and the popular vote used to elect the president. This will never happen because the country would be bereft without that extra set of numbers to play around with.

Saturday, 1 November

The mechanical side of voting in the US is receiving full attention, as it always does several days before an election. Remember the hanging chad? The machines used and the requirements for voting vary from state to state; it's an insane patchwork of dubious reliability. If the outcome of an election is a landslide, well and good, but any close race can be called suspect, hence all the recounting and lawyers from both parties in attendance at polling stations. Efforts to regularise the system always fail because the voting apparatus is in the control of the states, and that means political patronage. A sticker in Ohio, where the election outcome was dodgy in 2004, sums up the inefficiency of the system: "I Think I Voted."

This year the usual worry about malfunctioning voting machines and the deliberate and malicious spread of misinformation has turned into out-and-out alarm because of the enormous surge in voter registration. An example of misinformation: if you are in foreclosure, you can't vote. Another: Your home address and driver's licence have to match. Neither is true. Here in New York, 100,000 early votes got sent to the wrong location, and it's unsure if they can be retrieved. Another vexing problem is the introduction of electronic voting machines – DREs – that are susceptible to viruses and hacking.

The good news is that early voting, usually used by the old and infirm, is attracting thousands who want to avoid long lines on election day and those who have to work Tuesday. A quarter of those eligible have already cast their votes. Oprah made news by casting her vote early: an electronic vote. She didn't press the button hard enough or pressed it too hard – and her presidential vote wasn't registered. I think I voted. Her advice: double-check.

While New Yorkers refuse to count the presidential chicken before it hatches, we are going full bore on predicting who will fill cabinet positions in an Obama administration. A parlour game of sorts.

I dine with Australian friends. One of their guests is a semi-retired accountant knowledgeable about securitisation. I explain to him that entire units at many major US banks and insurance companies had no board oversight, no limits on leverage, no risk management, few or no capital requirements, inadequate accounting. Taken together, no under-standing of risk and not, as many financial experts are arguing, a mis-reading of it.

Makes no sense, but that's what happened. He doesn't believe me. Looks at me like I'm a nutter.

On a trip to Australia in May, I repeatedly puzzled aloud at the spending down of the surplus that Kevin Rudd had inherited when a worldwide economic downturn was looming. Even blind Freddie, or the politically correct equivalent thereof, must know this. The response: Australia had no subprime problems. Not subprime, I'd say, the fall-out from subprime. So goes the United States, so goes the rest of the world. And the reaction again was as if I were not a Cassandra but a nutter.

I was often told that Australia will be fine because its fortunes are hitched to China, an unstoppable economic power. But China is still an autocratic communist country and one that wields blunt economic instruments. And it might not be quite so unstoppable. I've heard that at least 15,000 plants have closed in China in the last few months, a fact which its ever-secretive leadership has been at pains to hide. This helps with the tainted food and toy problem, but not much else.

Sunday, 2 November

Dick Cheney endorses John McCain. Cheney's approval ratings are at 18 per cent, lower even than Bush's. With friends like these ... After he gives his endorsement, Cheney has a throaty coughing fit. Something sticking in his craw?

Sales of assault weapons are booming in states with liberal gun-control laws because of fears that Obama will ban them. And you never know, you might need a semi-automatic rifle with a commie running the country.

Ceaseless door-knocking and relentless phone-calling is going on all over the nation. The Obama campaign is not allowing one voter to go unturned.

Going through my notes, I am cheered by an auto-worker in Michigan who said of Obama, "I don't care if he's polka-dot as long as he can get us out of this mess."

Monday, 3 November

Kathy, an art-dealer friend, describes for me the experience of canvassing for Obama in Philadelphia's Ward 26, a ghetto neighbourhood that is black and Hispanic but also heavily Catholic. Lots of undecideds because of the abortion issue. Invariably the first question would be about Obama's pro-choice stand. Kathy would explain that he didn't like the idea of abortions at all. Instead, he wanted to start a major effort to reduce unwanted pregnancies. She would then turn the conversation to the economy or Iraq. Several black men told her that they would not vote for Obama just because he was black. Fair enough. A few doors were slammed in her face, along with a stream of not-so-fleeting invective. But nearly all the conversations finished with the householder saying, "Have a blessed day," not something we hear in New York.

Kathy was also sent to a Republican suburb that she says was like the set from The Truman Show. The experience was downright weird. No cars, no children playing, no dogs being walked, no music or television sounds issuing from houses. And no one answering their door. But people were inside. She could see movement.

The *Christian Science Monitor* runs a heart-warming piece by Jonathan Curley, an undecided voter who was persuaded by his wife to tag along while she canvassed for Obama:

> There has been a lot of speculation that Barack Obama might win the election due to his better "ground game" and superior campaign organization. I had the chance to view that organization up close this month when I canvassed for him. I'm not sure I learned much about his chances, but I learned a lot about myself and about this election.
>
> Let me make it clear: I'm pretty conservative. I grew up in the suburbs. I voted for George H.W. Bush twice, and his son once. I was disappointed when Bill Clinton won, and disappointed he couldn't run again. I encouraged my son to join the military. I was proud of him in Afghanistan, and happy when he came home, and angry when he was recalled because of the invasion of Iraq. I'm white, 55, I live in the South and I'm definitely going to get a bigger tax bill if Obama wins.
>
> I am the dreaded swing voter.
>
> So you can imagine my surprise when my wife suggested we spend a Saturday morning canvassing for Obama. I have never canvassed for any candidate. But I did, of course, what most middle-aged married men do: what I was told. At the Obama headquarters, we stood in a group to receive our instructions. I wasn't the oldest, but close, and the youngest was maybe in high school. I watched a campaign organizer match up a young black man who looked to be college age with a white guy about my age to canvas together. It should not have been a big thing, but the beauty of the image did not escape me.
>
> Instead of walking the tree-lined streets near our home, my wife and I were instructed to canvass a housing project. A middle-aged

white couple with clipboards could not look more out of place in this predominantly black neighborhood.

We knocked on doors and voices from behind carefully locked doors shouted, "Who is it?"

"We're from the Obama campaign," we'd answer. And just like that doors opened and folks with wide smiles came out on the porch to talk.

Grandmothers kept one hand on their grandchildren and made sure they had all the information they needed for their son or daughter to vote for the first time. Young people came to the door rubbing sleep from their eyes to find out where they could vote early, to make sure their vote got counted. We knocked on every door we could find and checked off every name on our list. We did our job, but Obama may not have been the one who got the most out of the day's work.

I learned in just those three hours that this election is not about what we think of as the "big things." It's not about taxes. I'm pretty sure mine are going to go up no matter who is elected. It's not about foreign policy. I think we'll figure out a way to get out of Iraq and Afghanistan no matter which party controls the White House, mostly because the people who live there don't want us there any-more. I don't see either of the candidates as having all the answers.

I've learned that this election is about the heart of America. It's about the young people who are losing hope and the old people who have been forgotten. It's about those who have worked all their lives and never fully realized the promise of America, but see that promise for their grandchildren in Barack Obama. The poor see a chance, when they often have few. I saw hope in the eyes and faces in those doorways.

My wife and I went out last weekend to knock on more doors. But this time, not because it was her idea. I don't know what it's going to do for the Obama campaign, but it's doing a lot for me.

Tuesday, 4 November

Dancing in the streets if Obama wins. Rioting if not. I can't believe Obama won't win – those long lines at polling booths from coast to coast aren't Republicans – but this is a bloody-minded, unpredictable country.

Much blather on the networks that we are on "the precipice of history." I vote at the High School for the Performing Arts behind Lincoln Center. It's a tiny polling centre, only two booths. And the machines are the antiquated lever type that are so old that if you push the lever hard enough, or so the joke goes, you might end up voting for Coolidge. But they are reliable, even if a mechanic has to be called in now and again. I have only a short wait but the polling staff say they were besieged earlier in the day, before the work day began.

Obama wins. A landslide. Highest voter turnout since 1960, when John Kennedy electrified the nation with his youth and optimism. Obama's victory speech is pitch-perfect, shot through with echoes of Lincoln, FDR, JFK and Martin Luther King. His words are inspiring but sobering: "The road ahead will be long. Our climb will be steep. There will be setbacks and false starts." The intensity with which people listen to him scores my brain, impresses me even more than the speech itself. "Here comes everybody," yes, and they have a hunger for a leadership that believes in a capacious common good, a need for a decisive break with the incestuous politics and sulphurous practices that have characterised Washington in the past forty years.

Serendipity, maybe, but Obama gives his acceptance speech in Chicago's Grant Park, where anti-war protesters and police clashed violently at the 1968 Democratic Convention. The year that hope died in the United States. And now, forty years later, by electing Barack Obama, young people and people of ordinary good will are again believing that they can change the United States.

The television networks are justifiably in raptures about the historic election of an African-American as the president. All the same, while it is astonishing that a man of colour could be elected president, given hundreds of years of vicious racial discrimination, to reduce Obama to a label, to "African-American," does him – and us – a disservice. He wasn't elected for the colour of his skin; he was elected because he offered the hope of a wise, steady and healing leadership to a country bullied and battered in the name of patriotism, plundered and pillaged in the name of free markets, neglected and abandoned in the name of small government.

More to the point, Obama is an extraordinary stew of ethnicity and influences – Kenya, Indonesia, Kansas, Hawaii. He's our first post-colonial world leader. Maybe even our first post-ideological leader, unless you count being a progressive as an ideological stance rather than one indicating common sense. As I watch him I want more than anything for my husband to have lived to see this moment. He was a Southern boy who was himself a racial blend, a hodgepodge of similar hopes and yearnings. And a beneficiary of and believer in FDR's New Deal. And then I remember my young nephew and niece, Harry and Ya-Ya, likewise a dazzling mixture, and I smile.

Karl Rove agrees with me! Rove is now a screaming head on Fox News. He thinks everyone is making too much of the election of an African-American to the presidency. Why, we got beyond race a long time ago, says Rove. In fact we've already had a black first family: the Cosbys. He's not joking.

Immediately after Obama leaves the stage at Grant Park, we hear from black politicians but not from anyone representing the rest of us – the polka-dots. And not from the college kids who were the foot-soldiers, the first and truest believers in the possibilities presented by an Obama presidency.

Obama doesn't forget them, though. The minute that it was clear he had enough Electoral College votes to become president, an email with the subject line *How This Happened* goes out to every last person who donated to his campaign:

I'm about to head to Grant Park to talk to everyone gathered there, but I wanted to write to you first.

We just made history.

And I don't want you to forget how we did it.

You made history every single day during this campaign – every day you knocked on doors, made a donation, or talked to your family, friends, and neighbors about why you believe it's time for change.

I want to thank all of you who gave your time, talent, and passion to this campaign.

We have a lot of work to do to get our country back on track, and I'll be in touch soon about what comes next.

But I want to be very clear about one thing …

All of this happened because of you.

Thank you,

Barack

His campaign rarely missed a beat, and neither will his administration.

The day after the election, the New York Times had a one-word headline: OBAMA. The stock market ratcheted downward. Dmitry Medvedev, the Russian president, ordered the deployment of nuclear-capable missiles on Poland's border for the first time since the Cold War. An international incident sooner rather than later.

The next day, I attend with three of my women friends – a Palinesque shout-out to Sue, Kathy and Nancy – a taping of The Daily Show. A fitting end to an era, or so we thought. Before the taping begins, Jon Stewart always takes questions. I don't have a question – I just want to say thank you for getting us through the past eight years – but my friends scotch that idea: too soppy. Uncharacteristically soppy.

There has been some worry that Stewart will have trouble finding humour in an Obama administration. But comedy material didn't vanish – poof! – on Tuesday. To wit a clip that Stewart used of Gordon Brown, plonker to end all plonkers, commenting on Obama's victory: "This is a moment that will live in history as long as history books are written."

At the end of the taping, Stewart says what a pleasure it is to do shows in front of happy audiences. Not soppy, just sincere. And we are happy. Giddy! The euphoria hasn't worn off. I am marvelling at how a country's mood can change from despair to hope overnight. Walter, a screenwriter friend and also a World War II veteran, remarks that the only time he can remember a similar outpouring of joy and a nationwide sense of relief was on VE Day.

Then and now, singing and dancing. Our mood isn't affected by the announcement that so far in 2008 1.2 million workers have lost their jobs, with most of the shucking occurring in the last three months. And I shrug off the news that condo prices in my immediate neighborhood are up 25 per cent. Some of that bailout money, no doubt, making our world even brighter and guiltier. My private soundtrack has been Beth Orton's cover of "Ooh Child": *Ooh-oo child, things are gonna get easier /*

Ooh-oo child, things'll get brighter. And Leonard Cohen's "Anthem": *Ring the bells that still can ring / ... There is a crack in everything / That's how the light gets in.* What a year we've had!

New York City, 7 November 2008

Acknowledgements

"Who You Callin' a Maverick" by John Schwartz. From *The New York Times*, 4 October 2008 © 2008 The New York Times. All rights reserved. Used by permission and protected by the Copyright Laws of the United States. The printing, copying, redistribution, or retransmission of the Material without express written permission is prohibited.

"Obama & Sweet Potato Pie" by Mark Danner is reprinted with permission from *The New York Review of Books*. Copyright © 2008 NYREV, Inc.

"My wife made me canvass for Obama; here's what I learned" by Jonathan Curley is reprinted with permission from 3 November 2008 issue of *The Christian Science Monitor* (http://www.csmonitor.com). © 2008 The Christian Science Monitor. All rights reserved. For permissions, contact copyright@csmonitor.com.

Peter Cosier

Tim Flannery is a fear-mongering, doom-laden "Alarmist of the Year" in his environmental commentary and interpretation of climate-change science.

That's what his critics would have you believe. Take this statement, for example: "On the balance of probabilities, the failure of our generation on climate-change mitigation would lead to consequences that would haunt humanity until the end of time."

The trouble is, that's not a Flannery quote, it's a quote from Professor Ross Garnaut, one of the most eminent economic reformers of modern Australia, in his final report, released in September this year: the *Garnaut Climate Change Review*.

You don't need to read Flannery to become alarmed at climate change, you just need to read the science.

What puts Tim Flannery at the cutting edge of the climate-change debate is his predisposition to conceptualise and visualise unknown worlds, core to his palaeontology background. He might have rocks in his head, but he is far from crazy. He knows the past and looks to the future.

This is what sets Tim Flannery apart – his ability to see through time and to communicate this future. He is able to see across generations. He can visualise our world in fifty years, and this vision haunts him.

With every hit he receives, he probably wants to put his head in the sand like a good palaeontologist and leave us to it. Instead, he feels his responsibility acutely and the storyteller in him sends him out again and again to spread the word.

The truth is that a future of unmitigated climate change really will haunt humanity until the end of time. The world's climate scientists tell us that we need to keep greenhouse gas concentrations in our atmosphere below 450ppm CO_2e (carbon-dioxide equivalent) if we are to have even a 50 per cent chance of keeping global warming below a critical threshold of 2 degrees above pre-industrial levels.

Professor Garnaut says that Australia's share of a 450ppm agreement would involve reducing emissions in the order of 25 per cent by 2020 and 90 per cent by 2050.

The implications of a global stabilisation target of 450ppm for Australia and the world are simple, but profound. No matter which phase in the industrial revolution countries are in, we are going to have to completely decarbonise the world's energy-production systems and we are going to have to restore a positive carbon balance in the world's natural landscapes – our forests and our agricultural lands – and we have forty years to do it. You can understand Tim's urgency.

We need to reframe the industrial revolution. We need to build a 21st-century economic system that is profoundly different to that of the nineteenth and twentieth centuries.

Yet while the political and technical challenges are enormous, we are finally coming to realise just how economically feasible this is. In the early years, business can make a profit and households can save money when they invest in technologies such as building insulation, fuel efficiency and solar water heating. With the exception of currently unproven carbon capture and storage technologies, we actually have all the technologies in place today to fix the problem. Professor Garnaut is unequivocal: "the cost of action is less than the costs of inaction."

The graph below highlights the implications of achieving a 450ppm CO_2e target for the Australian economy. It is based on Australian Treasury projections of future economic growth in Australia.

The grey line shows the explosion in wealth expected between now and the end of this century if GDP continues to grow in the order of 1.5 per cent per capita per annum.

The black line shows you what a reduction in GDP really means if we commit to stabilising greenhouse gas concentrations at 450 ppm CO_2e by 2050.

No sane human being would risk runaway climate change on the basis of this information.

This graph should be on T-shirts because it conveys a most hopeful message: a price on carbon will drive the next industrial revolution.

While the mitigation of energy generation is a must-do if we are to have any chance of achieving such a target, this focus has masked the many opportunities for Australia to harness the power of restoring terrestrial carbon (biosequestration).

The solution to climate change has not one, but three components:

—Energy technology (to produce carbon-pollution-free energy) – this needs to provide 50 per cent of the solution;

—Energy efficiency (using less energy and in the process saving money) – 25 per cent;

—Landscape management (we need to let nature help us, because trees and soils absorb carbon) – 25 per cent.

Landscapes absorb vast quantities of carbon, so by reducing land clearing and increasing carbon stocks through revegetation and soil carbon, landscape management can become a fundamental part of controlling the CO_2 balance in the atmosphere.

Restoring terrestrial carbon by managing our landscapes is a very different approach from emissions reductions because it actually makes a positive contribution to stabilising the world's climate system by drawing carbon pollution out of the air. This is an unbelievably important concept. Healthy landscapes can

Australian Economic Growth 1800 AD to 2100 AD

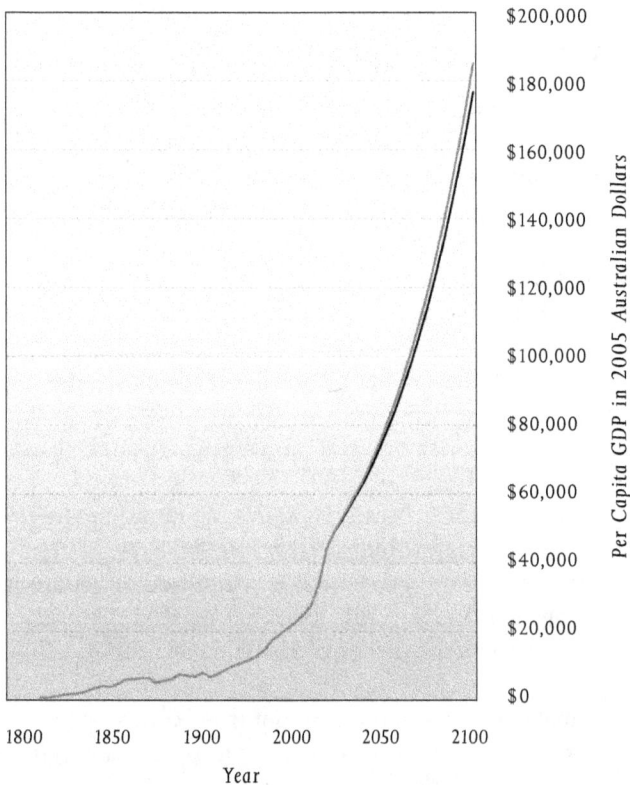

(Wentworth Group of Concerned Scientists www.wentworthgroup.org)

become more valuable than cleared ones because rainforests and restored river basins store vast quantities of carbon.

The scale of this opportunity globally is almost unimaginably large. Even a small gain is of enormous significance. Just one of a dozen bio-sequestration opportunities currently available has the potential to reduce Australia's annual emissions by over 50 per cent each year for the next fifty years. Ross Garnaut agrees. He believes that that full utilisation of bio-sequestration could "favourably transform the economic prospects of large parts of remote rural Australia."

Investments for storing carbon in terrestrial landscapes can be targeted to produce multiple environmental and economic benefits. For example, restoring native vegetation along the nation's rivers, wetlands and estuaries would improve water quality and re-connect native vegetation across our vast, fragmented landscapes. In addition, it would increase soil carbon in agricultural landscapes, which improves the productivity of our soils, which have been in slow decline over the past two centuries.

There is one other great economic and institutional reform that we must embrace, one which on face value seems a little mundane compared to the other two of decarbonising the world's energy-production systems and putting an economic value on landscapes that draw and store carbon from the atmosphere, but it is one that lies at the very heart of our current environmental problems.

We are now aware that our future prosperity is linked to effective stewardship of nature: our land and water, a stable climate, clean air, healthy coasts and marine resources. We now know that without stable, functioning natural systems, our economic prosperity is transient and intergenerational financial security is a mirage. We are in the early stages of the twenty-first century, yet our environmental accounting practices are in the Dark Ages. If you can't measure it, you can't manage it.

It is one of the great failures of public policy of our generation and it is at the core of our environmental problems. It has resulted in policy and land-use decisions that have caused significant and unnecessary damage to our natural environment, and it has resulted in the massive waste of billions of dollars of public funds aimed at repairing this damage.

Australia needs to confront the challenge of managing our natural capital with the same discipline with which we manage our economy. Australia needs an environmental accounting system, including carbon accounts, that will inform government, business and community decision-making.

Building the National Environmental Accounts of Australia will change the way we manage Australia: the design of our cities, how and where we produce our food and fibre, and how we direct public and private investments as we strive to improve and maintain the health of our environmental assets.

Today we wouldn't dream of managing the economy without rigorous accounting standards for our personal accounts, for business dealings and for managing the national economy. Environmental accounts are fundamental to dealing successfully with the 21st-century challenges of stabilising the world's climate systems and managing nature.

With three great reforms – decarbonising the world's energy production systems; putting an economic value on landscapes that draw and store carbon from the atmosphere; and building environmental accounts – our generation has the opportunity to transform the economics of the 21st-century, and in doing so, transform the management of nature and, with it, our place in history.

But as Tim Flannery so brutally puts it, there is no time to lose.

Peter Cosier

Richard Branson

With scientific gravitas, complemented by the skilful use of layman's language, Tim Flannery paints a serious picture of the planet's future, even if, as he says, he overwhelms us "with the scale and the number of challenges facing humanity."

Let me start with a huge dose of optimism. I believe that we will rise to the challenges Tim poses. I believe it is possible that one day we will enjoy modern, fun-filled lives using only one planet's worth of natural resources. We will emit minute amounts of carbon, there will be radically less evidence of poverty, and most people, most of the time, will enjoy healthy, satisfying lives. Sustainability is possible. If I have been successful, it's because I believe the impossible is possible and I have, in my business life, made it so. Okay, building a business is not saving the planet, but we all need that same "let's do it" attitude if we are going to see this challenge through.

As a businessman responsible for nurturing companies, careers and customers, as well as meeting environmental and social responsibilities, I find the major challenges, particularly climate change and food production, almost too vast to contemplate. At the moment, the tone of voice around sustainability implies sacrifice and giving stuff up. Unsurprisingly, consumers reject this because it seems to present fewer opportunities for a satisfying life. We know the opposite needs to be true. To this end, the world's experts could join us in a bigger debate about lifestyle choices and lifestyle possibilities.

None of us can afford to be reluctant to comprehend the scale of change required. We need to get ready for drastic as well as piecemeal action. I don't deny that we have all been guilty in the past of ducking the issue. Governments and politicians, by their nature, think in the short term, to the next election in democratic countries at least. Businesses have to meet the demands of their shareholders, who want short-term as well as long-term profit. Consumers – the general public – fret about the lives of their children or their grandchildren, but as individuals they feel powerless to do anything and question the difference it would make if they did.

I believe there is still a gap between the way business leaders think and the way environmental experts, such as Tim, think. Business people consider the laws of economics, while Tim considers the laws of nature. These two sets of laws are not natural bedfellows. The fundamental challenge facing us all is to make the necessary and important rules by which we run our economy complement the laws of nature. The laws of economics were created in modern history to serve mankind, whereas the laws of nature go back billions of years and serve the entire ecosystem on which we rely. Therefore, while the laws of economics matter, they cannot overrule the laws of nature, and perhaps that is the humble pie Tim is inviting us to eat.

I am, however, heartened by a growing realisation that businesses, governments and citizens can form a powerful triumvirate to act in concert. While there are squabbles and disagreements, there is also a movement supporting the best academic and scientific brains, as well as admired statesmen, in the belief that "something has to be done." Initiatives such as the "Elders" and the "Environmental War Room" are indications of this, each aiming to find solutions to global environmental and social challenges. The purpose of the War Room is to evaluate major solutions to climate change and to create incentives to enable their rapid and scaled deployment.

Tim Flannery deals with the macro issues facing society, and my businesses can and will make an important contribution to these. We will strive to understand where our products help provide short- and long-term contributions while reducing the negative contributions. It is complex. It is easy to be harsh on the family flying to the Caribbean on the grounds of the carbon emissions that result, but what about the benefit to the local communities and the benefit of quality family time? And what about the members of our health clubs – is their desire to keep fit a positive contribution in its own right? How can our mobile communications help rural and inaccessible communities? Patently, Virgin Group companies can make a positive or negative contribution towards making sustainable lifestyles easier, and each of them is being asked to identify what those contributions may be.

The questions we are asking our companies go beyond the usual corporate social responsibility puff and KPIs that some big businesses are expected to measure. Yes, we do measure our carbon footprint; yes, we do recycle and reduce waste; yes, we do invest in the latest, most fuel-efficient planes. But we also ask broader questions such as: what does an economy that only uses the resources of a single planet look like? How do we decouple economic growth from the use of natural resources? How do we contribute to lives powered by clean and renewable energy?

We are a business, so commercial success is foremost in our mind. But we also ask ourselves how we can ensure that the basics of the free-market economy will still operate, albeit with rules that are better aligned with the laws of nature.

Tim Flannery points out the power of tropical rainforests and their need for protection. The tropical rainforests are home to an estimated two-thirds of all living species and to hundreds of millions of people and, as he emphasises, to some of the world's most unsustainable agricultural practices. Like Tim Flannery, we believe that perhaps the biggest single opportunity that links the need to address poverty in developing countries and the need to reduce the rate of climate change is reversing the rapid and unsustainable rate of deforestation.

To do this, we need to ensure that rainforests are worth more alive than dead. So another question we ask ourselves is this: what influence can we have on developing creative ways of giving financial value to eco-services provided by rainforests and oceans to ensure that the economy will work within the finite limits of nature? At the moment, a rainforest generates more income when it has been converted into garden benches and oil palm. How do we create more income by leaving the original forest standing?

One of the Virgin companies – Virgin in the UK together with Virgin Unite – has just begun working with the Climate Tree, an initiative of the Tropical Forest Trust, helping to finance a project in the Congo to find entrepreneurial ways of helping local people create value from their forests without causing damage.

Some readers might be bristling, annoyed by my focus on rainforests when airlines are meant to be one of the most evil perpetrators of climate change, but as a journalist from the UK *Independent* commenting on the UK Stern Report wrote last year:

> It is unwise for politicians to arm-wrestle over rising aircraft emissions when just the next five years of carbon emissions from burning rainforests will be greater than all the emissions from air travel since the Wright Brothers to at least 2025.

IT has also easily overtaken aviation as a source of greenhouse gas emissions (half a billion servers and growing). However, aviation is still seen as high profile and is coming under emissions-trading schemes. There are proposals in both Europe and Australia. Naturally I would prefer a single global scheme, but either way these schemes will generate billions of dollars. I believe that some of this money should be channelled into projects to protect rainforests.

It is not just about carbon and rainforests. Wellbeing is an important element of a sustainable lifestyle. A generally wealthier population in the Western world has not always led to increased happiness and wellbeing. Instead there has been an increase in obesity and stress levels, as well as in diseases such as diabetes. So we are debating how our businesses can ensure that self-esteem and pleasure are based more on experience and the realisation of one's potential than on the ownership of more and more stuff. We also ask how we can help people extend their personal wellbeing into community wellbeing. In many cases, the solution is simple: recycle more, keep fit and buy greener products.

This does not discount the need to find large-scale technical solutions, and initiatives such as the Earth Challenge (a US$25-million prize to encourage a viable technology that will remove at least one billion tonnes of atmospheric CO_2 equivalent per year) will make hugely important contributions. These solutions, along with the development of non-fossil-generated energy and the major challenge of containing population growth, are all part of the bigger picture of true sustainability.

While I hope these questions we are asking show some robust intellectual thinking, I am also aware that more action on the ground is required. We will continue to work with partners more expert than us to ensure we are tracking in the right direction; we will ensure that new investments contribute to, rather than work against, achieving sustainable lifestyles; we will resource our own experts and reinforce the knowledge of these issues among our senior managers; and we will encourage our businesses to be leaders in their sectors.

While the future challenges are massive and, at times, the outlook seems bleak, I persist in seeing the glass as half-full. To sit on the sidelines is to place our way of life at risk and possibly see millions of people die of starvation or suffer from extreme weather conditions. Such a prospect is what provides the impetus to act and to act now. No single group can solve the problem, which is why we need to work together, whether as individuals, businesses, governments or NGOs, to reach creative, pragmatic yet bold decisions that will create tipping points for the challenges we face.

Some might think I am too optimistic. However, I would rather be optimistic and proved wrong than pessimistic and proved right. That's entrepreneurialism for you and I know a little about that. Just imagine a world where the best scientists collaborate with the best entrepreneurs – perhaps then my optimistic vision will become reality.

Richard Branson

David Foster

Gaia is anomalous. As living beings, we cannot hope to explain life through our statistical sciences because anomalous singularity lies beyond our scientific purview.

To deploy the language of statistical mechanics, life is improbable. When a planet's gaseous atmosphere is probable (i.e. observed in a state of thermodynamic equilibrium), that planet has lost if ever it possessed a capacity for thermostasis – in James Lovelock's mind, the *sine qua non* of planetary life. But a system cannot understand itself through reason alone. In the short term, it is human civilisations at risk here and, moving from science to history, these civilisations, if history is any guide, are in a bad way. Flannery makes the point that burgeoning human population threatens human civilisations. Climate change, as geochemist Lovelock implies, is best seen as Gaia's response to human hubris, for, if we move from science to theology, in order to avail ourselves of the proper language for discussing life, we can observe that if anything is certain, it is that human hubris, in the form of technological innovation, has led to the ever-decreasing human death rate and ever-increasing consumption of fossil fuels, in regard to which we have behaved (to quote another chemist, Cornforth) with all the restraint of a fox in a chicken coop.

It is surely poignant that Tim Flannery's essay *Now or Never* opens a *Quarterly Essay* concluding in correspondence arising from Paul Toohey's *Last Drinks*. This serves to remind of the complete resistibility – even among Australians possessed of survival skills – of a voluntary, secular reversion to the lowest of all possible ecological profiles – that of the hunter-gatherer. The problem, in other words, isn't one of communication but, rather, of motivation. Even if climate sceptics prove correct, a move towards frugality would do Australians no harm. This we understand, but we also suspect that such transformation will not occur, should it require the deliberate collapse of the world economy with the pre-consent of over half the world population. There are half a billion Indians presently living a Gandhian rural life, but the ever-expanding urban slums of India suggest that only a saint remains content subsisting off a hectare, in the face of ubiquitous multi-channel cable television. It is the well-heeled urban intellectual to whom the Gandhian lifestyle appeals. The villager wants none of it.

Most of us, proffered a choice between illicit comfort and doing it tough, will opt for comfort, in deed if not word; *a fortiori*, given the plaudits attending the pursuit of both eminence and wealth.

I have tried, for almost forty years, to live a sustainable rural life. It is hard going, swimming against the stream, and I'm about done. My wife and I even published a book on self-sufficiency (*Slow Food*, Duffy and Snellgrove, 2001). It is, at the end of the day, a dispiriting undertaking, so permit me a smile at Flannery's endorsement of "holistic management" in beef cattle, which sounds rather like dairy farming without the dairy. Permit me a smile at Michael Pollan enthusing over Polyface Farm (Pollan, incidentally, for those who wish to read further, can certainly write: Lovelock, sadly, can't). And I smile, not because such innovative systems can't be made to work: it's more a question of who's going to put their hand up.

Where does the water come from in this "holistic management" scheme? Who's going to drive the solar-powered water tanker, or do we use the windmill? Who's going to monitor fencing round that feedlot with no feed? Hungry steers break electric tapes. Who's going to grow all the silage? Hungry cattle lose condition. No breeder in his right mind would run bulls with heifers. To fetch top dollar we need to AI then preg test all those cows, Tim; surely you can't be denying us the technological state of our art? That would be pretty rich, coming from you. So who's going to shift, every few days, and in between growing the silage, the tread-ins with the energisers, the silage feeder, the water tanker, the mobile trough, the mobile yards, the mobile race, the mobile crush – the missus? She prefers, these days, to jump into her car. A modern woman does not like work that involves taking orders from a husband. Even accepting suggestions, the kids? Long gone to the city. Employees? No money to pay them: we're not all merchant bankers. Extended family? You're joking. Contemporary partners of sons and daughters baulk at living with in-laws. In fine, your typical Australian farm-force: one old man with an overdraft and a limp.

The hunter-gatherer lifestyle, the lifestyle of the nomadic horde (which remains the stock-breeding paragon), even the life of the peasant farmer, is predicated on sexual differentiation and reliant on extended family – *utterly reliant*. You can't do it on your own but you will be. In the face of digital "propensity for individualism," as Kim Mahood calls it, clan in the West is all but kaput.

But I bring Good News. There is glamour in poverty. It is simply hard to see through all that haze. There is happiness in release. There is meaning in frugality and purpose in celibacy. Sell the cattle to India to comfort the five million saddhus. Eat grass. The human race has long possessed a safety valve in the face of utter failure. It is undertaken instinctively on acceptance of a renunciant faith. In the past, when under duress, men and women of every stamp – Chinese, Egyptians, Tibetans, Greeks, Ethiopians, Irishmen – have renounced the devil and all his pomps to retreat from a collapsing world in response to heartfelt remorse. Scientists, in general, disapprove of faith, and contemporary dogma needs a touch-up, but the impulse to rediscover God is not yet dead in humankind. We must, perhaps, become a trifle warmer yet, but a Dark Age is good for some things.

Bring it on.

David Foster

Geoff Russell

I wrote to Tim Flannery in July 2005 when he was at the South Australian Museum. The CSIRO *Balancing Act* report had just shown that Australia's meat industry was a bigger generator of greenhouse emissions than our entire transport sector, so I reasoned that he might seriously consider a call for all South Australian Museum food-service areas to become meat-free zones. I expected McDonald's role as a museum sponsor might create an obstacle, but I wasn't prepared for the tenor of Flannery's response. He announced himself a "proud eater of flesh" and requested I not contact him further.

In the intervening years Flannery has written an entire book about climate change, *The Weather Makers*, without any acknowledgment that Australia's livestock produce more warming than its coal-fired power stations. He has written an editorial in *New Scientist* railing against the 700 gigalitres of water used by our coal-fired power stations while ignoring the 7000 used by our beef and dairy industries. A recent study examined 4582 climate-change articles in US newspapers between September 2005 and January 2008 and found that Flannery's blinkers are widely worn, with just 0.5 per cent mentioning food animal emissions, despite these being larger than those from transport.[1]

But Flannery has now decided in *Now or Never* to talk about livestock publicly. He has livestock, cattle in particular, duck into a phone box and emerge transformed in cape and tights as not only the guardians of cool, the mop and bucket to our fossil-fuel slops, but also the saviours of the world's starving. Flannery wants a return to mixed farming and an expansion of the livestock industry in the world's rangelands.

Flannery's plan departs from mainstream scientific consensus in many ways. Rajendra Pachauri, the head of the IPCC, recently gave a major speech, "The Impact of Meat Production and Consumption on Climate Change," calling for global reductions in meat consumption. He cited as major reasons for this the methane and nitrous oxide produced, and the deforestation associated with the production of livestock and livestock feed. Also worrying is the fossil-fuel intensity of the meat-production chain. The 2006 United Nations report *Livestock's Long Shadow* paints a detailed picture of an industry that is fouling every part of our planetary nest. This is pretty much the opposite of Flannery's vision.

Also at odds with Flannery is the man he calls "arguably the world's greatest climate scientist," James Hansen. Hansen thinks that meat reduction is the second most important thing that any individual can do to combat climate change. What is his number one action? Simple – elect the right government, one that will declare a moratorium and eventual phase-out of coal. Australia is yet to find out if rejecting the wrong government is the same as electing the right one.

Even more surprising than Flannery's retreat from scientific consensus on the contribution of the livestock industries to greenhouse gas emissions is his silence on an industry that has done more to destroy the tropical forests of the world than any other. Flannery is consistent in his use of "agriculture" to mean cropping and uses the term "pastoralism" or "grazing" when he is talking about livestock, so we can see that his blinkers are firmly in place when he identifies the culprits destroying the world's tropical forests:

> Today, mechanised tropical forestry and agricultural practices
> greatly amplify the destruction, with the result that the tropics are
> full of grasslands that are of little use to anyone ... It is only the
> loggers ... who benefit.

According to the 2006 United Nations report mentioned above, 70 per cent of Amazon deforestation is put down to cattle. Brazil is double the combined size of the eleven countries making up South-East Asia, so what happens in Brazil dominates tropical averages and generalisations. There are now 207 million cattle in Brazil. Most of the beef is supplied to various South American countries who have elevated pride in meat eating to heights that even Flannery couldn't scale. Where does logging rank? It accounts for about 3 per cent of Amazon deforestation. In Africa, logging is a major player, but the rates of tropical deforestation are tiny compared to Brazil.

Indonesia is the second biggest destroyer of tropical forests after Brazil. It is about the same size as Queensland with about the same number of cattle – 11 million. But Indonesia has 237 million people! The Indonesian data is sketchy, but the Queensland cattle industry deforested over 400,000 hectares per annum in the late 1990s to house its cattle and Indonesia's cattle have to live somewhere. It's either cut down forests or build more feedlots. Neither mixed farms nor rangelands are an option.

Flannery apparently wants Brazilian and other cowboys throughout the tropics to sit in front of computers and trade carbon emissions and give up fun things like branding cattle, lighting fires and knocking down trees. Why they would do this voluntarily is beyond me. If steak is good enough for Tim Flannery, Al Gore, George Bush and Kevin Rudd, then who is going to tell them to trade an axe for a keyboard?

The man who is Flannery's guide in his plan to increase cattle on the world's rangelands is rancher Allan Savory. Savory believes it's a myth that "desertification is caused by overstocking and overgrazing by livestock."[2] He also thinks it a myth that cattle are responsible for more greenhouse gases than automobiles, saying:

> The research data vilifying cattle has been obtained from mainstream, industrial, feedlot agriculture operations. There is an enormous distinction between animals in factory settings overfed on grains they did not evolve to eat and animals grazing on ranges as they evolved to do.

There is indeed a huge difference in the methane emissions of grass-fed cattle and grain-fed cattle, but Savory has got it the wrong way round. The CSIRO may not have tested Savory's magic holistic cattle, but they have tested Australian cattle on grass and grain, and those on grass produce about three times more methane.

The second difference between grass- and grain-fed cattle is the amount of meat you get. Grass-fed cattle in Australia and South America generate a carcase of 200 to 250 kilograms, while a grain-fed monster in the US will yield 350 kilograms. So a move away from feedlot cattle would slash the global cattle yield while increasing methane. To determine the net greenhouse impact would require an estimate of the fossil-fuel savings due to reduced grain inputs. Unlike Flannery, I won't just assume the net impact will be positive – that is a matter for calculation, not guesswork.

It's worth noting that the 2006 United Nations report contains a detailed map of land-use areas with high suitability for pasture but which are not being currently used as pasture. It is all forest or cropland with tiny pockets of urban areas. The bottom line is that the cattle industry has nowhere to go without causing more deforestation.

Savory, as I implied above, has his own theory on what causes desertification. Here are his words: "People assume that removing the livestock would allow the land to recover, but in reality, the complete removal of livestock accelerates the process of desertification."[3] Flannery thinks differently and argues: "if the rangelands were to be destocked and left unmanaged, it is likely that fire would burn the vegetation, which would lead to more carbon entering the atmosphere and huge increases in nitrous oxide."

Once more Flannery rejects science. In particular, he is rejecting the basic scientific understanding of the carbon cycle. A grassland grows by taking in carbon dioxide and turning it into grass (with the help of soil nutrients). If you burn the grass, the carbon dioxide is released, and other gases are also produced – like the nitrous oxide that Flannery mentions. Go back in twelve months and the grass is back with as much embodied carbon from the same source as before. There is no net carbon-dioxide emission to the atmosphere. In the case of a forest fire, the cycle takes a little longer but the principle is the same. It is only when a fire changes a landscape permanently that there is a net emission of carbon dioxide.

However, Flannery is right about the nitrous oxide. The release of nitrous oxide and some other gases isn't balanced. Most plants don't pull any nitrogen from the air, and those that do (via microbes inside their roots) pull free nitrogen not nitrous oxide.

In various media interviews since his essay was released, Flannery has claimed that science holds the key to mitigating climate change. I couldn't agree more, but Flannery is happy to hook up with a person who rejects empirical scientific data relating to both overstocking as a cause of land degradation and the role of livestock in methane production.

Flannery dresses up his meat agenda with concern for the global food crisis and calls for a return to more traditional mixed farming based on a farm made famous by New York Times journalist and author Michael Pollan. The cover of Pollan's 2008 book In Defense of Food is adorned with a lettuce that carries his motto: "Eat food, not too much, mostly plants." Vegan he is not, but Pollan is far closer to the vegan end of the spectrum than to the end that advocates a diet of wildebeest washed down with blood and yoghurt. In this latest book he writes: "Thomas Jefferson probably had the right idea when he recommended using meat more as a flavour principle than as a main course, treating it as a condiment for the vegetables."

Let's do the maths on the "abundance" of food that Polyface produces. Flannery lists the output with palpable awe: 25,000 pounds of beef, 25,000 pounds of pork, 1000 turkeys, 10,000 broiler chickens, and some loose change in rabbits and eggs.

In total, with generous rounding, Polyface produces 45 tonnes of food from 60 hectares per year. Is this an impressive output? An average Australian potato farmer would get 2160 tonnes from 60 hectares. Any plant food or collection of plant foods will wallop the productivity of Polyface. At the bottom end of the range, an almond farmer could get 60 tonnes from 60 hectares. If the meat figures are carcase weights, only 60–70 per cent is edible and 60 tonnes of almonds would provide about double the protein that Polyface produces. Most grains average around 2 tonnes per hectare, but rice can give you ten. If you grow all the food organically, then the output will drop, but it can never drop to anything remotely like the pitiful red and bloody output of Polyface farm. This is basic biology: there is less biomass as you go along any food chain.

It isn't explicit in his essay, but I'm guessing Flannery thinks there is something better about animal protein. But there are no practical differences between plant and animal protein. This is a myth longer and older than the rabbit-proof fence but with far more holes. The weapon of choice for malnourished children these days is a plant protein, fortified peanut butter, which works at least as well as the previously used fortified dairy products.

The UN's Food and Agriculture Organization allows us to summarise the efficiency of the world's animal food industry with a simple statistic. Animal food production consumes the output of one-third of all arable land, plus 3400 million hectares of additional grazing land, plus the entire and declining output of global fisheries, but produces a mere 17 per cent of global calories.

Flannery's description of the future of the planet if we don't act with extraordinary speed and commitment is as accurate as it is chilling. Here he is explicating the careful science of an army of researchers and doing it with his usual flare. But his excursion into the rocky waters of solutions shows that his dedication to science in the search for solutions is pretty thin. His desire to eat at the top of the food chain, come what may, when we can more healthily eat at the bottom, shows a deep reluctance to make even a minor culinary sacrifice for the sake of the planet he loves. Pachauri is right, Hansen is right, Flannery is simply wrong. Reducing meat production is an essential part of reducing our load on the planet.

Geoff Russell

1. Roni A. Neff, Iris L. Chan and Katherine Clegg Smith (2008), "Yesterday's Dinner, Tomorrow's Weather, Today's News? US Newspaper Coverage of Food System Contributions to Climate Change," in Public Health Nutrition, PreRelease (Y).
2. <www.holisticmanagement.org/n7/climate_07.html#cattle>
3. <www.greenuniversity.net/Ideas_to_Change_the_World/AllanSavory.htm>

Alanna Mitchell

I was jetlagged in Brisbane the first time I read Tim Flannery's splendid essay and originally I thought it was about Australians and Australia. But on reflection, I realised that it is an invocation to all humanity and that Flannery's homeland is an elegant metaphor for the planet as a whole.

It is a single system, after all, and we humans are a single, messy species. We are connected with each other and with everything else on Earth, despite all that our powerful tribalistic stories tell us to the contrary. The very plasma that courses through our veins has the same magical chemistry as the ocean's planet-blood that gave birth to life.

As his essay shows, few know the scope of this ineluctable connectedness better than Flannery. Few have sensed more deeply what will happen if the system lurches into a new, post-human mode. And Flannery is alone in his uncanny ability to explain what we can do to try to prevent that. All this has made him, in my view, the world's foremost oracle.

But as I sat in hotel room after hotel room through September, shifting to Sydney, Melbourne, Adelaide and finally Hobart, watching the world's financial institutions turn to puddles on the global trading floor, watching the American government try in vain to shape them up again and watching the panic escalate, I admit to sheer marvel at Flannery's sense of timing.

Here, written in trillions of dollars and billions of lives, were the makings of just such a system shift as Flannery has been telling us about. The meltdown is a searing example of the logarithmic system change that scientists predict for the biological world, played out in the language of money instead.

It wasn't neat and orderly. It was bewilderingly chaotic. It just kept going, throwing new curves at dazed observers. Here Lehman Brothers fell. There, the banking industry as a whole threatened to topple, leading to unknown consequences. Stocks lost trillions. Brokers, once great strutters, began to slouch and then to slither. That wash of money that investment bankers had seemed to handle so deftly had somehow taken on a mind of its own. What started out affecting millions grew to billions, and then to trillions. Suddenly, no one was immune. Terrified national governments conjured up hundreds of billions of dollars, scores of billions of pounds and euros to shore up the tidal wave. Had that money not materialised, the financial system was poised to morph into a different beast altogether.

This is the definition of system switch, the same phenomenon Flannery foretells in the realm of Gaia if we do not – quickly – step in.

Time will tell if the financial intervention worked. The principle, though, is sound: once a system begins to tilt, it takes heroic efforts to convince it not to shift merrily, heedlessly, catastrophically into something wholly new. And then you have to figure out what the causes of the breakdown were and also the trends underpinning the cause, and fix them. (This is where Nicolas Sarkozy, the French president, has come in so handy lately, talking about what the capitalist financial order was for in the first place.)

A couple of larger points emerge from the muddle. Some of the public discourse has been about whether we should now just hunker down and forget about going green, about investing in the sorts of world-saving technologies that Flannery tells us about in his essay. I heard it the other day in Toronto at a conference on corporate social responsibility. Maybe, a fellow or two opined, we should pull in our horns, stick to the old-fashioned assessment of risk, focus on the short term until the heavy weather clears. In other words, save a system just so it can crash again. Because, as is clear, the financial system nearly went under because it couldn't keep going under the same circumstances that had brought it to its knees. Something had to change. It wasn't sustainable. All that profligate profit was based on something that wasn't there.

So going brown, financially speaking, is precisely the wrong answer. This is, as Matthew Kiernan explained the other day, a "teaching moment." He is chief executive of Canada's Innovest Strategic Value Advisers and one of the braver souls at the Toronto conference. To him, the crash is a "trillion-dollar advertorial" for expanding the narrow, traditional definition of financial risk. In his view, assessing risk – and therefore opportunity – must include looking at elements such as environment, human rights, politics, labour markets and even health and safety practices. "The current paradigm is broken," he says. "What better moment?" The lesson is to keep going down the green financial road.

I think we could go further. What if the world's trillions in investments could be used to produce profit *as well as* social and environmental good? What if they were seen as two sides of the same coin and it were acknowledged that one was absent without the other? The planet's carbon-dioxide concentrations could be lowered swiftly and efficiently. It's not as crazy as it sounds and very smart financial people have been looking at this seriously, now that carbon has become a global commodity with a value. We are all one system. All of this is interconnected. Finance and biology are, in thought and deed, parts of a whole.

Flannery's timing is impeccable. Not only did his essay come out just at the moment when, for the first time in generations, all assumptions seemed to be collapsing; not only was the biological meltdown he refers to brought to life in the financial markets before our very eyes; not only are his Australian suggestions for breaking the untenable cycle a poignant recipe book for other countries; but the essay also, in its rich faith in humanity's ability to cope with the exigencies upon us, offers up the gift of poetry, and with it, the power of hope.

Alanna Mitchell

Ian Lowe

Tim Flannery is right to say that we face a planetary emergency. Climate change is not just a serious threat in itself, but also a factor compounding other major environmental problems like the catastrophic loss of biodiversity, increasing water shortages, the degradation of rural land and the decline of fisheries. Four reports in the UNEP series on Global Environmental Outlook, the Millennium Assessment and the report of the International Geosphere-Biosphere Program have all reached the same conclusion. As GEO2000 said, the present approach is not sustainable and postponing action is no longer an option. It has been clear for twenty years that the rate of burning fossil fuels poses the risk of dangerous interference to the global climate system. Our current situation has been made unnecessarily difficult by decades of government inaction, largely driven by a naive faith in market forces and, until last year, our national government's studied refusal to accept what the science was clearly saying.

Meeting our global responsibility for climate change demands rapid reduction in carbon-dioxide emissions. The fourth IPCC report, released last year, urged the big polluters like us to reduce our emissions 25 to 40 per cent by 2020, as part of a reduction of at least 80 per cent by 2050. More recent science suggests that these targets may not be enough to prevent dangerous climate change. A cautious approach that recognises the uncertainty of the science would lead to greater reductions. Some are suggesting we should aim for a 50 per cent cut by 2020 and 95 per cent – effectively decarbonisation – by 2050. Any serious targets will require attention to electricity supply and use, transport and agriculture. The other big problem looming, "peak oil," compounds the difficulty of shaping a coherent policy. As with climate change, we have known for decades about the problem, but decision-makers have been in denial. Some alternative transport fuels that looked promising, such as shale oil, tar sands and liquid fuels from coal, are now effectively ruled out by the need to reduce our release of carbon dioxide.

So what should be the basis of our response? We need the sort of serious targets specified above and a comprehensive approach to the whole issue. As the prime minister said in his closing speech to the 2020 Summit, "Climate change is the overarching issue this generation and those to follow must address." He concluded that climate change should be considered in all decisions. I agree. It should, for example, have informed the recent response to turmoil in financial markets. As Tim Flannery correctly observes, "While a high price for carbon is absolutely necessary, it alone will not be sufficient." Recent events should have demonstrated beyond any doubt that it is irresponsible to leave an issue as important as the survival of civilisation to the capricious behaviour of markets. As well as a realistic price for carbon, certainly at least $50 per tonne, we also need serious targets for the share of our electricity from renewable sources, for appliance efficiency, for the performance of domestic and commercial buildings. We should also pay attention to urban planning, ensuring that the services people use often are within easy reach on foot or bicycle, as well as investing in a massive upgrade of public transport for longer journeys.

So far, I agree completely with Tim Flannery. Where I part company is on the issue of "clean coal," the new technological saviour now that nuclear power's feet of radioactive clay have been exposed. I just don't think it is realistic to put all our eggs in that very fragile basket. It is certainly true that we have to do something about the overwhelming dependence on coal for electricity in this country. The biggest single contribution to climate change is carbon dioxide from burning coal, mainly to generate electricity. Coal is a very dirty fuel for two fundamental reasons. Because it always contains a range of impurities, burning it produces a cocktail of gases, like oxides of sulphur and nitrogen, as well as soot, ash and heavy metals, even some radioactivity! More basically, coal is mostly carbon, so burning coal gives carbon dioxide, the most important greenhouse gas. Oil and natural gas contain significant amounts of hydrogen, which burns to produce water. As a result, those fuels produce less CO_2 per unit of energy. Brown coal has a third problem: as it is mostly water, most of the energy produced by burning is used to evaporate the water. It thus gives even less useful energy for every kilogram of CO_2 released.

So how could burning this dirty fuel be cleaned up? Some believe we could capture the CO_2 from burning coal, compress it into a liquid and inject that into rock layers deep underground. This does nothing to reduce the other forms of pollution, so talk of "clean coal" is the height of chutzpah. Because air is nearly 80 per cent nitrogen and only about 20 per cent oxygen, CO_2 is only a small fraction of the exhaust gases from a power station. Separating it from the other gases is complex, expensive and takes large amounts of energy. Some propose burning coal in pure oxygen rather than air, so the exhaust stream would be mainly CO_2. That would simplify separating the CO_2, but it would be expensive and energy-intensive to produce enough oxygen to burn bulk quantities of coal. Compressing the gas into a liquid is technically feasible, but it also takes large amounts of energy. The liquid CO_2 would then have to be transported to sites where the rocks are judged suitable for storage. The World Energy Council has estimated that the CO_2 from the world's power stations would, if compressed to liquid for transport, be a volume comparable with the entire global oil and gas industry! While there are some sites that look suitable for long-term storage, it has not yet been shown that they would be secure for geological time; obviously, we could not afford to have the gas leak out into the air. There may be some sites secure enough and close enough to power stations for a few demonstration projects, but it is pure moonshine to believe this approach could be applied to all future power stations.

Even if all the technical problems could be solved, the extra energy required for the process would mean that CO_2 released per unit of energy would only be reduced by about 70 per cent. We need to go much further than this by 2050 to stabilise the global climate, so it makes much more sense to invest in the really clean forms of energy, such as wind, solar and geothermal. There are no credible estimates of the possible cost of carbon capture and storage, but industry sources talk openly about it possibly adding 50 per cent to the price of coal-fired power. Tim Flannery suggests that a carbon price as high as $80 per tonne might be needed for "clean coal" to be economic. Studies of the prospective renewable-supply systems show they could achieve greater reductions at lower cost – and much faster. Even if everything were to work as well as the optimists hope, it would be many years before the technology could be credible. The most that could be claimed is that "clean coal" might perhaps slow the growth of greenhouse pollution after 2020. Climate science is now saying we face an emergency and need to cut emissions significantly before then. While the whole idea is still unproven, even if it could be made to work it would do too little, too slowly and at too high a cost. So why is it being taken seriously?

There is no simple answer. Coal companies want to stay in business, so they have an obvious commercial reason to claim that we can keep burning coal. At the 2020 Summit earlier this year, I said that there are differences of opinion about the feasibility of "clean coal," but we could surely all now agree that it is irresponsible to continue "dirty coal" by building old-fashioned coal-fired power stations. A few delegates, mainly from the industry, objected – so Senator Wong had to report that there was no consensus for the position I advocated. I was shocked to find that there are still people in the coal industry who think it is acceptable to plan projects that will belch out millions of tonnes of CO_2. As well as business interests, some unionists representing coal workers – and some ALP politicians close to those unions – support "clean coal." The companies think it would be acceptable to keep the Earth habitable if it doesn't reduce their profits; the labour interests think it would be acceptable if no jobs are lost. To be fair, jobs are at stake. The coal industry, domestic and export, employs more than 25,000 people. To put that figure into perspective, while John Howard was prime minister 150,000 jobs were lost from manufacturing. In other words, the average annual loss of manufacturing jobs was about half the total employment in the coal industry. Those workers were absorbed by other fields of employment. Expanding clean energy supply and efficient use will create far more jobs than the coal industry now provides. Training and other forms of assistance would help the workforce move into the more satisfying jobs that would be created.

Some technocrats still hope for a big technical fix to the problem of climate change. So they are attracted to grand technical delusions like "clean coal" or nuclear power, rather than accepting the wisdom of applying simpler technologies, such as wind turbines, solar cells or improved efficiency.

The final complexity is the level of political support, including public endorsements and huge allocations of funds. Even politicians who accept that climate change is a real and urgent problem are reluctant to propose the changes we need. They cling to the old myths: that business can go on as usual, that further growth is tolerable, even that growth should be encouraged. We are now seeing a concerted campaign by some industry interests to dilute still further the Garnaut report's recommendations for an emissions trading scheme. Garnaut has supported a very gentle start to the scheme, with prices as low as $20 per tonne of carbon, but vested interests are clamouring to be sheltered even from this charge. A report released by the Australian Conservation Foundation calculated that the proposed public support of "trade-exposed industries" would cost the taxpayer billions, most of which would be hand-outs to very profitable overseas-owned corporations which employ relatively few Australians. This is wasting money we should be using to stimulate the new industries needed to meet our reduction targets. As Tim Flannery points out, a carbon price of $40 per tonne would probably make bio-char economically feasible. Various studies have concluded that a range of renewable-supply technologies would be economic at $50 per tonne. We should face up to the need to completely re-invent our electricity system over the next forty years so it will have been decarbonised by 2050. That will require both a realistic price for carbon emissions and a range of other government support measures.

I criticised the Howard government for pursuing the ridiculous distraction of nuclear power rather than responding to climate change. The equally simplistic notion of "clean coal" is now playing a similar role for the Rudd government and state governments along the eastern seaboard: it is a simulated response, aimed at appeasing the public concern about climate change without antagonising business, unions or those troglodytes in parliament who still can't see the problem. This is the real danger of the "clean coal" bandwagon. It is frittering away the time and resources that we should be using to re-structure our energy supply and use. The Rudd government should trust us and engage the community in developing a concerted response strategy, as was done in Sweden. We need that sort of participative process to produce a politically sustainable strategy to slow climate change. Unless we achieve that, we all face a very bleak future.

The fundamental message of Tim Flannery's essay is that we need to recognise the limits of ecological systems and build that recognition into our planning. Allowing markets to decide how resources will be used and how waste products will be managed is ethically indefensible. It means that selfish wishes of today's affluent minorities take precedence over the needs of all future generations. We also need to get over our universal fixation on growth. There is no prospect of a sustainable future unless we stabilise the human population and our per capita consumption at levels within the capacity of the biosphere. I agree with Tim Flannery that we should utilise geothermal energy, but I would not support the idea of a massive mineral-processing industry in the Cooper Basin. We already face the prospect of a lunar landscape stretching for a hundred kilometres or more if the bizarre plan to expand the Olympic Dam mine goes ahead. In a carbon-constrained world, it makes no sense to base our economic future on exporting huge volumes of low-value commodities. We should instead be investing in the growth industries of the twenty-first century, such as clean energy supply, efficient energy use and water-efficient food production.

Ian Lowe

Barney Foran

On a late July midday this year, I sat in a Beechworth meeting hall packed to the rafters to hear Tim Flannery present the essence of *Now or Never* to a regional audience. Every year we have "a name" blow in to town to present the Kerferd Oration, to honour the memory of George Kerferd, one of the town's founding fathers. We all turn out. Some do because they must, some come to be seen, but most of us come out of interest. There was a sizeable minority from the regional universities, government departments and NGOs who knew the message well enough, and wouldn't be too critical. The majority, though, needed convincing. Flannery might have been "Australian of the Year" and have written more books than can be found in the local library, but we're all equal down here. To convince the locals, the orator requires just the right mix of logic, humility and persuasion.

How Flannery won us over was through the simplicity of his message delivered in big metaphorical lumps: Earth's three organs (crust, water, atmosphere), the way humans are good at solving pollution problems, and the complex interactions that allowed the human species to develop here and which in turn we are rapidly undoing. Flannery's central tenet is that humans will soon need to take control of the planet's metabolism or endanger civilisation's survival. On the day he convinced us, but will his solutions work to keep us sufficiently distant from the point of no return?

I'm interested in the two Flannerys I saw on the podium that day. First is Flannery the Scientist/Integrator, who we know through science and his landmark books *The Future Eaters* and *The Weather Makers*. Second is Flannery the Advocate/ Politician, who must force change in the philosophies and actions of corporations and governments. The second requires flexibility and losing an occasional battle to secure the end-game. This duality increases the audience but also the critics. In particular, our national flat-earth broadsheet, the *Australian*, frequently regales its sceptics with the times that Flannery has backtracked on clean coal, nuclear and other core beliefs found in the conventional-wisdom tool-kit. How does this essay reveal the two Flannerys? Do we accept the words of both of them and does the message remain intact throughout?

As one who reads the same literature as Flannery, I found that two things stood out. The Scientist/Integrator in him has a powerful grasp of the science and its essential meaning. It is one thing to read the last ten papers of NASA's James Hansen but another to compose a sentence that gives the main message and puts to one side the waves of uncertainty that wrack the normal brain. To do this correctly and robustly is a rare achievement. Even more intriguing and impressive is Flannery's intellectual background of archaeology, human endeavour, colonial history and pure "fur and feathers" biology. When he writes about what we stand to lose, he knows bone by bone what we've already lost, and can prove that our demise is accelerating.

In this essay Flannery importantly gives us hope with his Geothermias, forests and feedlots, internet-based carbon trading with tropical-forest owners, and pyrolysis. Engaging solutions, which obviously work better than today's policy mishmash, produce an upwelling of desire for this imagined new world. In his "Revolution in the Feedlot" section I became intrigued with the stories from Polyface Farm and the "ecological sculpting" (what wonderful words) that provides a diverse flow of tasty nutritious produce on less than one-third of the farm. His Geothermia does not quite work for me, but the technological parts therein are factual and feasible. Perhaps the Advocate/Politician is saying that every town in every region needs to become its own Geothermia.

Rereading *Now or Never* several times reminded me again of Flannery's power as a writer and the triumph of his metaphors. The everyday scientist in me would try to win the readers over with graphs and tables, footnotes and proof. Flannery has these at his disposal, but his proof is very much a weight-of-evidence one, a much richer tapestry in which every sentence and word has many layers of meaning, and proofs within proofs. Challenge him and I know you'll get another essay on that point. This is perhaps the best part of the Advocate/Politician in him. Such is the distilled wisdom carried in his words, the orator's bombast and tricks are not required. The words themselves carry the day.

The Advocate/Politician in Flannery maintains the "clean coal" illusion and we must ask why? Perhaps travels to India and China and experiencing the latent expectations there have backed him into that dark corner. Unfortunately, widespread deployment of clean coal has a parasitic feedback that physically impedes the economic system it is trying to save. It's a bit like going for line honours in the Sydney to Hobart while towing ten wheelie bins full of empty champers bottles from a profligate run-in into Christmas. The University of Manitoba's Vaclav Smil, a Flannery-like big thinker on technologies, notes the impossible physical task that clean coal requires. Capturing and storing just one-tenth of the world's CO_2 emissions each year would "have to force underground every year a volume of liquid (compressed gas) larger than the volume of crude oil extracted globally by the entire petroleum industry." Smil views this as physically and economically impossible and suggests we bite the bullet and leapfrog immediately into renewable energy.

Flannery is correct to promote the promise of pyrolysis technologies for carbon storage and fuel production. If he blended the need for forests with the need for pyrolysis, the solution could help save Australia's farming communities and farmed landscapes. The core insight is the need to replace fossil carbon with biological carbon, particularly for our transport fuels. In 2050, an Australia with 40–60 million hectares under farmed forests and wood crops could be self-sufficient in liquid fuels and escape the growing trade imposts of imported oil. Regional processing hubs or "energy-plexes" could make fuel, bio-electricity, bio-char for carbon storage and soil improvement, and green chemicals. Centrally, these tree crops can integrate a changing climate much better than current cropping systems. The regional jobs and economic value-adding derived would remake rural Australia.

Combining pyrolysis for fuels with renewable-electricity technologies gives us the renewable-energy economy. Our modelling shows that this approach provides superior economic and greenhouse outcomes to the "conventional-wisdom" approach embraced by both major parties. In spite of high capital costs, the real economic rewards come when the transition is in place and we can chug along driven by the wind, the sun, plant growth and heat from the Earth's core. Our personal consumption of stuff must reduce its energy content, our utilities sector must become much larger in volume and value, while our industry must make and repair energy machines instead of churning out yet more stuff for landfill. Governments, or unions for that matter, never consider this approach in its entirety because "What would we do with our coal?"

So how does Flannery's Gaian romp compare with the Garnaut report's plan for saving the Platinum Age? Garnaut's Chapter 24, "Fateful Decisions," reveals that while the economist and the biologist may have a lifetime of differences and dissimilar world-views, they end up in the same paddock. Garnaut's last sentence says it all: "On the balance of probabilities, the failure of our generation [to solve the climate-change problem] would lead to consequences that would haunt humanity until the end of time."

Both Flannery and Garnaut place their ultimate faith in technology. Flannery trusts things he can touch and see: forests, pyrolysis and change down on the farm. Garnaut expects carbon capture to work and should it fail, has a "backstop technology" that fortuitously appears in 2065 or 2080 when a high carbon price catapults atmospheric cleansers into widespread deployment. Neither man tells us we must radically change our lifestyle.

So does Flannery the Advocate/Politician and Scientist/Integrator make his case for a human takeover of Gaia? A definite yes on the case, but a resounding no on our collective willingness to do so. As I write, the global "banksters" are pleading for calm and resolute action to save our economic system. Flannery is calmer than the banking headlines, but his message more chilling as he looks beyond the sightlines of the market to make the case for civilisation's survival.

In a tumultuous few weeks we've so far found $2000 billion worldwide to save the banksters so we can maintain growth – and therefore ultimately increase climate pressures. If ever the atmosphere needed the rest that only a good depression brings, it is now. Yesterday our federal government found $10 billion to boost the Harvey Norman economy for the Christmas splurge. This year's federal budget grudgingly allocated $500 million over six years ($83 million per year) for renewable energy, or $2.3 billion over five years ($460 million per year) for all things climate. Adding to climate pressure by maintaining consumption is thus twenty times more valued than climate saving.

By saving the economic system that has propelled us to this point, we could lose the climate. We can't grow and shrink at the same time. It's not physically possible.

Barney Foran

Barrie Pittock

Tim Flannery argues that a high price for carbon emissions is absolutely necessary, but that "rising fuel prices have done relatively little to drive efficiency or behavioural change." While I strongly agree with the former point, the latter is clearly not correct, either globally or in Australia. Demand for public transport is rising, sales of large cars are falling, and there is growing interest in small cars, including hybrid, all-electric and even compressed-air cars. The problem is the relative slowness of public and private enterprise in meeting these changing but foreseeable demands.

Tim's argument concerning the necessity for some application of so-called "clean coal technology" (wisely not a phrase he uses) has some weight, but he misses the point that no carbon capture and sequestration (CCS) technology yet invented is 100 per cent clean. The 2007 Intergovernmental Panel on Climate Change gives a figure of about 85 to 95 per cent efficiency in capturing CO_2, but that requires roughly 25 per cent more energy to produce. This means that the effective leaking is about 12.5 per cent (10 per cent of 125 per cent), so that each new power station with CCS emits about one-eighth that of the equivalent non-CCS station. Thus, to reduce emissions one needs to retrofit CCS to existing "dirty" power stations or retire the old ones. That must be a condition on any new coal-fired power station with CCS, and indeed within a few years on our coal exports.

Tim is quite right to ask why the coal industry, both mines and power generators, have not seriously invested in CCS research and development this decade if not earlier. The whole world was warned by scientists in the 1980s that CO_2 emissions were a problem, but large emitters chose not to believe the science was real. They are guilty of poor risk management of their own investments and deserve little sympathy, although the coal miners are more deserving of consideration. What the coal and power industries need to do now is divert most of their profits into research and development of CCS, or investment in renewable energy.

Apart from its very partial nature, CCS faces an impossible task in going large scale, as the global coal industry would need a CCS industry as large as the present oil industry just to dispose of its waste. In competition with a scaled-up, learn-as-you-go renewables industry, they would be uneconomic, and the sooner they realise this the better for them.

The geothermal city Tim advocates is interesting, but somewhat less realistic than simply building an electricity network to send renewable electricity from the Cooper Basin geothermal fields (and elsewhere) to the existing large consumers. This includes not just the major Australian cities but also existing remote energy-intensive mines, refineries and manufacturers, such as Olympic Dam and Roxby Downs, and various installations on the north-west coast. Another huge opportunity is an electrical grid extending to Darwin and on by high-voltage direct-current (HVDC) cable to join up with the Indonesian grid. HVDC cables are low loss and economical over thousands of kilometres. Our own Basslink cable is HVDC, and they form the basis of a European proposal to link Europe with solar and other renewable energy sources in North Africa and the Middle East. The need for a better electrical grid for renewable energy in Australia is highlighted in the *Garnaut Climate Change Review*'s final report. Solar thermal, other geothermal and even tidal power loom large as opportunities across remote parts of Australia.

Such a grid and network of large-scale renewable-energy installations could also be a prime source of local employment for Aborigines in desert Australia, where the Bushlight program has already installed local renewable-energy supplies in about 100 remote communities. It could also benefit inland towns such as Mildura and Euroa, where so-called "drought" and factory closures are creating unemployment.

Solar power should loom much larger in Australia's energy future. Australia has the technology for large-scale concentrating solar thermal power with thermal storage, and a huge potential with the world's greatest continental resource of solar radiation in our desert regions. Engineering company Worley Parsons has proposed a network of thirty-four solar thermal power stations, each generating some 240 megawatts in Australia. There is also the near prospect of solar photovoltaic (PV) power at one-tenth of present costs using new printed PV-sheeting technology from the US Nanosolar company, which already has a manufacturing plant in California supplying the market in Germany. And let's not forget that one of the largest suppliers of solar PV technology is a Chinese company, Suntech. Australia also has the highly efficient SLIVER solar PV technology about to be manufactured in Adelaide by Origin Energy.

Solar energy can also solve our water-supply problem in coastal regions or where there is slightly salty bore water. In my view no desalinisation plant should be built in Australia without a dedicated and paid-for solar, wind or other renewable power station to supply it with energy.

Tim's section on using forests to sequester carbon is fair enough, except that he compares the potential storage amounts with the existing amount in the atmosphere (200 gigatonnes of carbon, or GtC), rather than with the amounts likely to be injected into the atmosphere by 2100 under so-called business-as-usual scenarios, which range from 770 to 2540 GtC. Given, as Tim argues, that the amount is likely to be near the top of the range without massive changes from the more realistic of the business-as-usual scenarios, the contribution from forest storage is not so significant. Reforestation can make a significant contribution in the next few decades, but reductions in emissions relative to business-as-usual must play the main role.

The section on farming and its potential ability to sequester carbon in the soil is also useful, but suffers from the same problem of comparison with the existing carbon stock in the atmosphere rather than projected future business-as-usual emissions. Holistic management sounds great, but again we are talking about removing from the atmosphere about 200 GtC in total, compared to the much larger projected emissions by 2100. It will help, but it is not the main answer, which must be drastic reductions in emissions.

Reforestation and holistic farming do have the unique ability to take carbon out of the atmosphere, and that will be needed, but they do not solve the problem (as I am sure Tim would agree). It is likely that we will end up stabilising concentrations of greenhouse gases in the atmosphere well above safe levels, and will have to draw down those concentrations later. This will require both reforestation and holistic farming, but probably other means for taking carbon out of the atmosphere. Pyrolysis is one such method, but it will need to be done on a huge scale. It will not be farming in any conventional sense but rather large-scale biomass pyrolysis to generate energy and sequester the charcoal thus produced. Perhaps other means, such as artificial photosynthesis, will also become feasible and economic. Let us hope so.

Finally, Tim focuses on the challenge of sustainability, with passing references to greed and hopelessness. Psychologists tell me that there are three likely reactions to potential disaster: nihilism (it's all hopeless so let's enjoy ourselves while we can); fundamentalism (falling back on some rigid set of beliefs such as that God or the free market will save us); or activism (the belief that there is hope if we apply ourselves to the problem with sufficient urgency).

We are seeing just such a set of reactions to potential disaster in the current global economic crisis. Remarkably, it has shown that even the most dyed-in-the-wool free-market believers are wavering in their recitation of the deregulation mantra, and that politicians, with public support, are intervening in an unprecedentedly large way. If they can spend trillions of dollars saving the banks, they can do as much for the climate. Failure to do so would gravely affect the global economy, with food shortages, coastal flooding, mass refugees and worse. We have to make certain that the politicians understand that securing climate stability is at least as important to the economy as saving the banking system. Then we will see real solutions to climate change. There could even be a massive synergy here, with large investments in energy efficiency and low-carbon technologies being just the boost the economy needs. Tim's essay is a useful stimulus to addressing the vital connection between climate change and the troubled economic system.

Barrie Pittock

NOW OR NEVER	*Correspondence*

Gwynne Dyer

Tim Flannery's greatest virtue is the clarity of his arguments, but he was insufficiently explicit and radical in his conclusions – quite possibly for tactical reasons, because they are implicit in what he does choose to say.

He rightly says that within the lifetimes of many readers, "Gaia will pass from an unconscious to a conscious means of control [of the climate]." He is talking about us, of course, and at the end of his essay he does refer to one deliberate human intervention in the climate that has got considerable publicity in the past two years: Paul Crutzen's proposal to inject sulphur into the stratosphere as an emergency preventive measure if global warming is getting out of control. But he does not admit (though I suspect that he really knows) that direct human manipulation of the fundamental elements in the climatic equation – the amount of greenhouse gases in the atmosphere and the amount of sunlight reaching the Earth's surface – is the way that things are going to be done from now on.

It is almost never acknowledged, in debates about how we prevent unfavourable climate change, that we are actually seeking to preserve one particular climatic state, desirable to human beings, out of a number of alternative possible climates that have prevailed in the past and may recur in the future. Certainly will recur, in the case of another period of major glaciation, unless we eventually use our newly acquired ability to manipulate the climate to prevent it. Does anybody imagine that a successor civilisation several thousand years hence, the beneficiary of our successful attempt in this era to avoid a global warming catastrophe, would not use the climate-control techniques we are developing right now to avoid a global cooling catastrophe as changes in the Earth's orbital pattern bring the current interglacial period to its natural end?

I may seem to be getting ahead of myself here, since it is far from certain that we will be successful in the present era in avoiding what would be, for human civilisation, a catastrophic amount of global warming. Jim Lovelock is quite right to fear that a failure of political will could lead to a tenfold reduction in the human population by the end of this century. But we should be clear about the nature of our task: our agricultural and industrial practices, magnified by our huge rise in numbers, are driving the global climate in a direction that will hurt us very badly, and so our task is to change those practices in ways that drive the climate back into our preferred equilibrium. We are already manipulating the climate by our activities; success will be manipulating it in more intelligent ways in order to serve our ends.

Whether you want to dress that up as human beings becoming the consciousness of Gaia, or just see us as the same old self-serving species we always were, we are taking control of the planet's climate. This billions-strong human civilisation will live or die by its success in understanding the global carbon cycle and modifying it as necessary to preserve our preferred climate. That is really what Flannery is talking about in his discussion of restoration of the tropical forests, the use of "bio-char" in agriculture, and the holistic management of rangelands: ways of bringing the atmospheric concentration of carbon dioxide back down below the ultimately disastrous level that it has *already* reached.

The consensus in climate-science circles is that we must never exceed a ceiling of two degrees hotter, because somewhere between two and three degrees hotter we will trigger natural feedbacks, most notably methane releases from melting permafrost and a collapse in the carbon-dioxide absorption by the oceans, which would unleash runaway warming and remove the situation from human ability to control. Two degrees hotter is generally equated to an atmospheric concentration of 450 parts per million of carbon dioxide – but Jim Hansen's most recent estimate of the acceptable *long-term* concentration of carbon dioxide in the atmosphere, if we do not want all the ice on the planet to melt, is 350 parts per million. That is rather worrisome, since we are already at 385 ppm and are almost bound to reach 450 ppm before the level stabilises, even if we get very serious very soon about cutting our greenhouse gas emissions.

We cannot afford to stay at 450 ppm for very long: there is a grace period of only a few decades before the consequent warming in the climate leads to irreversible changes, including the eventual melting of all the world's ice. The various agricultural and forestry changes that Flannery discusses will be of great use in getting that extra carbon dioxide back out of the atmosphere in the long run – but it is quite a long run, almost certainly longer than the time available if that level of carbon dioxide is allowed to translate into an equivalent rise in temperature.

But that does not have to happen. The dirty little secret is that we know of several techniques for keeping the global average temperature down, even though the carbon-dioxide concentration implies a hotter planet. These are not long-term solutions because they do nothing to slow ocean acidification and do not necessarily produce cooling in the parts of the planet that need it most, but as stop-gap measures to keep us from breaking through the two-degree barrier they are probably going to be indispensable for a while. They may be the only way that we can win extra time to work on getting our emissions down without breaching the limits and hitting runaway warming.

Flannery knows this, and even makes reference to one possible geo-engineering technique – Crutzen's sulphur-in-the-stratosphere proposal – but I do not think he gives the subject the prominence it deserves. These are techniques that may be crucial to our chances of getting through this without a calamity of global proportions, and they need to be researched and tested aggressively now. We may find that we need them quite soon.

Gwynne Dyer

Tim Flannery

Among the published responses to my *Quarterly Essay*, there is general agreement on the key point that the climate system is approaching crisis and that urgent action, on a scale not yet contemplated politically, is now required. Yet several respondents disagree on what actions should be taken.

David Foster doubts that anyone could or would want to take up holistic management because of the (imagined) great workload involved. In fact, the labour involved in holistic management is about equivalent to that on more traditionally managed properties, though work is more evenly spread throughout the year. Around 10 million acres worldwide are already managed this way, and the technique is spreading.

Geoff Russell takes exception to my suggestions for making animal husbandry more sustainable, presumably because he believes that humans should stop eating meat, regardless of whether it's sustainably produced or not. Yet it is undeniable that both meat and vegetable foods can be produced sustainably, or unsustainably, depending upon the methods used. For example, both soybeans and meat produced on newly cleared Amazonian rainforests are unsustainable, while sustainably harvested kangaroo meat and organically grown vegetables can be produced at no cost to the environment. I find it difficult to understand why Russell ignores my concluding remarks that "We should be eating what is good for the planet, as well as what is good for ourselves," unless it be from some moral repugnance of me as a "proud eater of (sustainably produced) flesh." If that is the case then an irreconcilable philosophical difference exists between us, in which sustainability is merely a sideshow.

Broader concerns from respondents centre on my proposals for "clean coal" technologies and my call for the development of the inland city "Geothermia." Barney Foran asks why I "maintain the clean-coal illusion" and speculates that "Perhaps travels to India and China and experiencing the latent expectations

there have backed him into that dark corner." He is quite correct. Australia may well be able to do without clean coal, but China cannot, and neither can China pay for it. That presents us Australians, who enrich ourselves by exporting coal on a colossal scale, with a difficult moral dilemma. Most resolutely opposed to "clean coal" is Ian Lowe, who believes that the approach cannot be made to work in a cost-effective manner, and that in pursuing it we will lose the opportunity to invest in other low-emissions energy alternatives such as solar, wind and geothermal. Lowe is rightly awed by the scale of the task, and I agree that retrofitting every coal-fired power plant with carbon capture is implausible. But a significant percentage of new plants in places like India and China must be converted.

It is my belief that the coal industry itself has made the search for "clean coal" solutions more difficult than it should be, for in pursuing solutions such as the now defunct US FutureGen project, which was to deploy Integrated Gasification Combined Cycle Carbon Capture and Storage, they have set out to develop a Rolls-Royce solution that is necessarily decades away. Approaches such as CS Energy's OxyFuel Project at the Callide Power Station in Biloela, Queensland, are far simpler and more cost-effective. Basically, CS Energy hopes to burn the coal in a mixture of 20 per cent oxygen and recirculated waste gases from the combustion process to create a high concentration of CO_2, which can then be compressed and sequestered. It's a technology that looks set to add a modest $30 per megawatt hour to costs, and which, with appropriate investment now, could be widely deployed in just a few years. My fear is that the industry doesn't want solutions like this to become available in the near future. Perhaps a carbon-trading scheme with a significant price for carbon will change their minds.

But where is the money for such technologies to come from? I'm indignant that the federal government is pouring buckets of my tax money into an industry worth $55 billion per year, and which is reaping record profits. If its approach is to have a shred of moral authority, the federal government must force the coal industry as a whole to foot the lion's share of the bill for "clean coal" and, as a condition of receiving taxpayer funds, to set out strict timelines for its development.

I'm surprised at the extent of the uneasiness among respondents with my vision for Geothermia. Everyone seems to admire the sustainable-city development at Masdar in the UAE, but few, it seems, want a similar sustainable city in their own country. I was, however, extremely heartened by Barrie Pittock's proposal for a high-voltage direct-current cable linking Darwin with Indonesia. It represents the kind of visionary thinking required if we are to avoid a climatic catastrophe.

Several respondents drew parallels between the financial crisis and the looming climate crisis. None, however, pointed out that the world's "reserve bank" of coolness in this warming climate is Earth's ice caps. They have stored "coldness" in the form of ice for thousands of years. It's terrifying now to watch the easily accessible bits of that "capital" vanishing to critical levels, for once we have run through that buffer, we have no other central bank to look to for salvation. Surely we need action not tomorrow but today – indeed right now.

Tim Flannery

Richard Branson is founder and head of the Virgin group of companies.

Peter Cosier is director of the Wentworth Group of Concerned Scientists, who came together in 2002 to pursue reform in the management of Australia's land and water resources. He was deputy director-general of the NSW Department of Infrastructure, Planning and Natural Resources and, for six years, a policy adviser to former environment minister Robert Hill.

Gwynne Dyer is a freelance journalist, columnist, broadcaster and lecturer on international affairs. He is the author of several books, including War, Future: Tense, The Mess They Made and Climate Wars.

Tim Flannery has published many scientific papers and more than a dozen books, including Throwim Way Leg, The Eternal Frontier, The Future Eaters, The Weather Makers and, most recently, An Explorer's Notebook. He chairs the Copenhagen Climate Council. A former director of the South Australian Museum, he is now based at Macquarie University. He was the 2007 Australian of the Year.

Barney Foran led CSIRO teams that reported on human population (Future Dilemmas), marine fisheries (Fish Futures), land and water (Decision Points) and life cycles of the whole economy (Balancing Act). He is a research fellow at Charles Sturt University, the Fenner School at ANU, and the physics department at the University of Sydney.

David Foster, University of Sydney medallist in inorganic chemistry and former international postdoctoral fellow of the US National Institutes of Health, won the 1997 Miles Franklin Award for The Glade within the Grove. His new novel, Sons of the Rumour, will be published in 2009.

Kate Jennings is a poet, essayist, short-story writer and novelist. Both her novels, Snake and Moral Hazard, were New York Times Notable Books of the Year. She has won the ALS Gold Medal, the Christina Stead Prize for fiction and the Adelaide Festival fiction prize. In the 1990s, she worked as a speechwriter on Wall Street. Stanley and Sophie, a memoir of life in New York City where she has made her home for the past three decades, was published in 2008.

Ian Lowe is emeritus professor of science, technology and society at Griffith University and president of the Australian Conservation Foundation. He studied engineering and science at the University of New South Wales and earned his doctorate in physics from the University of York. He is the author of many books, including *A Big Fix* and *Living in the Hothouse*.

Alanna Mitchell is the author of *Seasick: The Hidden Ecological Crisis of the Global Ocean* (2008) and *Dancing at the Dead Sea: Journey to the Heart of Environmental Crisis* (2005). She lives in Toronto.

Barrie Pittock retired as head of the CSIRO Climate Impact Group in 1999. His books include *Climate Change: Science, Impacts and Solutions* (second edition forthcoming in 2009) and the edited collection *Climate Change: An Australian Guide to the Science and Potential Impacts* (available at <http://greenhouse.gov.au/science/guide/index.html>).

Geoff Russell is a committee member of Animal Liberation (SA). He has written for the *Age*, *Dissent*, the *Monthly* and *Australasian Science*.

Subscribe to
QUARTERLY ESSAY

Subscriptions Receive a discount and never miss an issue. Mailed direct to your door.

☐ **1 year subscription** (4 issues): $49 a year within Australia incl. GST. Outside Australia $79.

☐ **2 year subscription** (8 issues): $95 a year within Australia incl. GST. Outside Australia $155.

* All prices include postage and handling.

Back Issues (Prices include postage and handling.)

☐ **QE 1** ($10.95) Robert Manne *In Denial*
☐ **QE 2** ($10.95) John Birmingham *Appeasing Jakarta*
☐ **QE 4** ($10.95) Don Watson *Rabbit Syndrome*
☐ **QE 5** ($12.95) Mungo MacCallum *Girt by Sea*
☐ **QE 6** ($12.95) John Button *Beyond Belief*
☐ **QE 7** ($12.95) John Martinkus *Paradise Betrayed*
☐ **QE 8** ($12.95) Amanda Lohrey *Groundswell*
☐ **QE 10** ($13.95) Gideon Haigh *Bad Company*
☐ **QE 11** ($13.95) Germaine Greer *Whitefella Jump Up*
☐ **QE 12** ($13.95) David Malouf *Made in England*
☐ **QE 13** ($13.95) Robert Manne with David Corlett *Sending Them Home*
☐ **QE 14** ($14.95) Paul McGeough *Mission Impossible*
☐ **QE 15** ($14.95) Margaret Simons *Latham's World*
☐ **QE 16** ($14.95) Raimond Gaita *Breach of Trust*
☐ **QE 17** ($14.95) John Hirst *"Kangaroo Court"*

☐ **QE 18** ($14.95) Gail Bell *The Worried Well*
☐ **QE 19** ($15.95) Judith Brett *Relaxed and Comfortable*
☐ **QE 20** ($15.95) John Birmingham *A Time for War*
☐ **QE 21** ($15.95) Clive Hamilton *What's Left?*
☐ **QE 22** ($15.95) Amanda Lohrey *Voting for Jesus*
☐ **QE 23** ($15.95) Inga Clendinnen *The History Question*
☐ **QE 24** ($15.95) Robyn Davidson *No Fixed Address*
☐ **QE 25** ($15.95) Peter Hartcher *Bipolar Nation*
☐ **QE 26** ($15.95) David Marr *His Master's Voice*
☐ **QE 27** ($15.95) Ian Lowe *Reaction Time*
☐ **QE 28** ($15.95) Judith Brett *Exit Right*
☐ **QE 29** ($16.95) Anne Manne *Love & Money*
☐ **QE30** ($16.95) Paul Toohey *Last Drinks*
☐ **QE31** ($16.95) Tim Flannery *Now or Never*

Payment Details I enclose a cheque/money order made out to Schwartz Media Pty Ltd. Please debit my credit card (Mastercard, Visa or Bankcard accepted).

Card No. ☐☐☐☐ ☐☐☐☐ ☐☐☐☐ ☐☐☐☐

Expiry date   /   Amount $

Cardholder's name   Signature

Name

Address

Email

Post or Fax this form to: Quarterly Essay, Reply Paid 79448, Melbourne, VIC 3000
Freecall: 1800 077 514 / Fax: 61 3 9654 2290 / Email: subscribe@blackincbooks.com

Subscribe online at **www.quarterlyessay.com**

www.ingramcontent.com/pod-product-compliance
Lightning Source LLC
Chambersburg PA
CBHW081401270326
41930CB00015B/3375